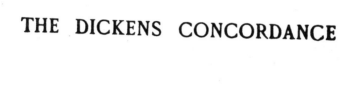

THE DICKENS CONCORDANCE

The Dickens Concordance

Being a Compendium of Names and Characters
and principal places mentioned in all the
Works of Charles Dickens

Containing first a List of the Works, secondly a Summary of
Chapters in each book or pamphlet, and thirdly a complete
Alphabetical Index of names, with the title of
book and number of chapter quoted.

BY

MARY WILLIAMS

FOLCROFT LIBRARY EDITIONS 1970

Limited to 150 Copies

The Dickens Concordance

Being a Compendium of Names and Characters
and principal places mentioned in all the
Works of Charles Dickens

Containing first a List of the Works, secondly a Summary of
Chapters in each book or pamphlet, and thirdly a complete
Alphabetical Index of names, with the title of
book and number of chapter quoted.

BY

MARY WILLIAMS

LONDON :

FRANCIS GRIFFITHS

34 MAIDEN LANE, STRAND, W.C.

1907

NOTE.

The letters f.m. refer to where a character is "first *mentioned*" but no *name* given until a later chapter.

The Contributions to the Christmas Numbers of Household Words for the years 1850, 1851, 1852, 1853 are included in Reprinted Pieces under the titles of " A Christmas Tree," 1850; " What Christmas Is, As We Grow Older," 1851; " The Poor Relation's Story, and The Child's Story," 1852; " The Schoolboy's Story and Nobody's Story," 1853.

CONTENTS

PART ONE

PAGE

LIST OF THE WORKS OF CHARLES DICKENS   .   .   .   1

PART TWO

LIST OF CHARACTERS AND PLACES IN THE ORDER OF THE
    BOOKS   7

PART THREE

COMPLETE ALPHABETICAL INDEX   .   .   .   ,   .   65

PART ONE

LIST OF THE WORKS OF CHARLES DICKENS

THE DICKENS CONCORDANCE

PART ONE

List of the Works of Charles Dickens

SKETCHES BY BOZ 1836
POSTHUMOUS PAPERS OF THE PICKWICK
    CLUB 1836-7
THE ADVENTURES OF OLIVER TWIST . . 1837-8
THE LIFE AND ADVENTURES OF NICHOLAS
    NICKLEBY 1838-9
MASTER HUMPHREY'S CLOCK 1840-1
THE OLD CURIOSITY SHOP 1840
BARNABY RUDGE : A Tale of the Riots of
    Eighty 1841
AMERICAN NOTES 1842
THE LIFE AND ADVENTURES OF MARTIN
    CHUZZLEWIT 1843-4
PICTURES FROM ITALY 1846
DOMBEY AND SON 1847-8
THE HISTORY OF DAVID COPPERFIELD . 1849-50

BLEAK HOUSE 1852-3
A CHILD'S HISTORY OF ENGLAND . . . 1852-4
HARD TIMES 1854
LITTLE DORRIT 1855-6
A TALE OF TWO CITIES 1859
GREAT EXPECTATIONS 1860-1
THE UNCOMMERCIAL TRAVELLER . . . 1860-9
OUR MUTUAL FRIEND 1864
THE MYSTERY OF EDWIN DROOD . . . 1870

MISCELLANEOUS PAPERS AND CHRISTMAS STORIES.

SUNDAY UNDER THREE HEADS 1836
THE MUDFOG PAPERS 1837
SKETCHES OF YOUNG GENTLEMEN . . . 1838
SKETCHES OF YOUNG COUPLES 1840

PLAYS.

THE VILLAGE COQUETTES 1836
THE STRANGE GENTLEMAN 1836
IS SHE HIS WIFE? OR SOMETHING SINGULAR 1837
THE LAMPLIGHTER 1838

Contributions to The Christmas Numbers of HOUSE-
HOLD WORDS and ALL THE YEAR ROUND,
including :
The Seven Poor Travellers 1854
The Holly Tree Inn 1855
The Wreck of the Golden Mary . . . 1856
The Perils of Certain English Prisoners . 1857

A House to Let 1858
The Haunted House 1859
A Message From the Sea 1860
Tom Tiddler's Ground 1861
Somebody's Luggage 1862
Mrs. Lirriper's Lodgings 1863
Mrs. Lirriper's Legacy 1864
Doctor Marigold's Prescriptions . . . 1865
Mugby Junction 1866
No Thoroughfare 1867

THE LAZY TOUR OF TWO IDLE APPRENTICES 1857
HUNTED DOWN 1860
A HOLIDAY ROMANCE 1868
GEORGE SILVERMAN'S EXPLANATION . . 1868

REPRINTED PIECES . . . .

CHRISTMAS BOOKS, containing
A Christmas Carol 1843
The Chimes 1844
The Cricket on the Hearth 1845
The Battle of Life 1846
The Haunted Man 1848

PART TWO

LIST OF CHARACTERS AND PLACES IN THE
ORDER OF THE BOOKS

PART TWO

List of Characters and Places in the Order

of the Books

SKETCHES BY BOZ, 1836.

OUR PARISH.

Chap. 1.—The Beadle, the Parish Engine, the Schoolmaster.—Simmons (Parish Beadle). Vestry. Parish Engine. Vestry Clerk. Master of the Workhouse. Our Schoolmaster.

Chap. 2.—The Curate, the Old Lady, the Half-pay Captain.—The Three Misses Brown. Goat and Boots Inn. Mr. Gubbins (ex-churchwarden). The new clergyman at Chapel of Ease. The old lady. Sarah, her maid. The Half-pay Naval Officer.

Chap. 3.—The Four Sisters.—The Four Misses Willis. Mr. Robinson. Mr. Dawson, the surgeon.

Chap. 4.—The Election for Beadle.—Captain Purday (f.m.2). Bung. Spruggins. Timkins.

Chap. 5.—The Broker's Man.—Fixem. Smith, (broker).

Chap. 6.—The Ladies' Society.—Mrs. Johnson Parker. Misses Parker. Mr. Henry Brown. The Missionary Speaker. Irish Pedlar ditto.

Chap. 7.—Our Next-Door-Neighbour.

SCENES.

Chap. 1.—The Streets—Morning.—The Servant of all work. Todd's Young Man. Betsy Clark and others.

Chap. 2.--The Streets—Night.—The Muffin Boy. Mrs. Macklin. Mrs. Walker. Mrs. Peplow. Mr. Smuggins and others.

Chap. 3.—Shops and Their Tenants.—The Draper. The Fancy Stationer. The Tobacconist and Bonnet-shape Maker. The Theatrical Hairdresser. The Greengrocer. The Tailor. Ladies' School. The Dairy.

Chap. 4.—Scotland Yard.

Chap. 5.—Seven Dials.

Chap. 6.—Meditations in Monmouth Street.— The suits of second-hand clothes.

Chap. 7.—Hackney Coach Stands.

Chap. 8.—Doctors Commons.—The Judge. Proctors. Registrar. Apparitor and Court-keeper. The Hand-bell Ringer. Counsel. Doctor of Law. Bumple and Sludberry. The Prerogative Office.

Chap. 9.—London Recreations. The wealthy City Man's Garden. The Middle-class Old Gentleman. The Tea Gardens.

Chap. 10.—The River.

Chap. 11.—Astley's.

Chap. 12.—Greenwich Fair.

Chap. 13.—Private Theatres.

Chap. 14.—Vauxhall Gardens by day.—Mr. Blackmore. Mr. Green and others.

Chap. 15.—Early Coaches.—Passengers. Guard. Ostler and Coachman.

Chap. 16.—Omnibuses.

Chap. 17.—The last Cab-Driver and the first Omnibus Cad. Mr. William Barker.

Chap. 18.—The House. A Parliamentary Sketch. Sir John Thomson. Mr. Smith. Officers. Reporters. Bellamys. Nicholas, the butler. Jane. Persons present.

Chap. 19.—Public Dinners.

Chap. 20.—The First of May. Sweeps and Jack in the Green. Mr. Sluffen.

Chap. 21.—Brokers' and Marine Store Shops.

Chap. 22.—Gin Shops.

Chap. 23.—The Pawnbroker's Shop. Mr. Henry. Mrs. Tatham. Mrs. Mackin. Jinkins.

Chap. 24.—Criminal Courts.

Chap. 25.—A Visit to Newgate.—The Turnkey. Old woman and her daughter, prisoner. The squalid-looking woman (prisoner) and her daughter (visitor). Women at dinner. Wardsmen and women. School for boys. Yard for men prisoners. The Chapel. The Pressroom. Condemned Cells.

CHARACTERS.

Chap. 1.—Thoughts about People.—The Poor Clerk.   The Clubman.   London Apprentices.

Chap. 2.—A Christmas Dinner.

Chap 3.—The New Year.—The Quadrille Party. The host, hostess, and daughters. Mr. Tupple. Mr. and Mrs. Dobble and other guests.

Chap. 4.—Miss Evans and the Eagle.—Mr. Samuel Wilkins, carpenter.   Jemima Evans, his sweetheart.   Mrs. Evans and two younger daughter.   Jemima's friends.

Chap. 5.—The Parlour Orator.—Mr. Wilson. Mr. Rogers and others.

Chap. 6.—The Hospital Patient.

Chap. 7.—The Misplaced Attachment of Mr. John Dounce.—Old Boys.   Mr. John Dounce. The Misses Dounce.   Messrs. Harris, Jennings, and Jones.   The young lady in blue.

Chap. 8.—The Mistaken Milliner.—Miss Amelia Martin.   Her friend who married the painter. Mr. and Mrs. Jennings Rodolph. Miss Julia Montague. Mr. Taplin.

Chap. 9.—The Dancing Academy.—Signor Billsmethi.   Master and Miss Billsmethi.   Mr. Augustus Cooper.

Chap. 10.—Shabby Genteel People.

Chap. 11.—Making a Night of it.—Mr. Thomas Potter and Robert Smithers.

Chap. 12.—The Prisoner's Van.

TALES.

Chap. 1.—The Boarding House.

1st.—Mrs. Tibbs, proprietress. Mr. Tibbs
Mrs. Maplesone, Matilda and Julia, her daughters.
Mr. Simpson. Mr. Calton. Mr. Septimus Hicks,
boarders. Robinson, maid servant. James, boy,

2nd.—Mrs. Bloss and servant, Agnes. Mr.
Gobler. Dr. Wosky, Mrs. Bloss' doctor. Mr.
Evenson. Mr. Wisbottle. Alfred Tomkins and
Frederick O'Bleary, other boarders.

Chap. 2.—Mr. Minns and his Cousin.—Mr.
Augustus Minns. Mr. Octavius Budden, his
cousin. Mrs. Amelia Budden. Master Alexander
Augustus Budden. Mr. Brogson. Mr. Jones, and
other visitors.

Chap. 3.—Sentiment.—Misses Amelia and Maria
Crumpton's school. Cornelius Brook Dingwall,
M.P. Mrs. Brook Dingwall and little boy. Miss
Brook Dingwall, Lavinia. Sir Alfred Muggs.
Emily Smithers and Caroline Wilson, pupils of Miss
Crumpton. Mr. Dadson, writing master, and wife.
Signor Lobskini, singing master. Mr. Hilton.
Theodosius Butler, alias Edward M'Neville Walter,
cousin of Misses Crumpton.

Chap. 4.—The Tuggs's at Ramsgate.—Mr.
Joseph Tuggs. Mrs. Tuggs. Mr. Cymon and
Miss Charlotte Tuggs. Mr. Cower. Captain
Walter Waters. Amelia. Jane, and other visitors.
Mrs. Belinda Waters. Lieutenant Slaughter.
The Tippin Family.

Chap. 5.—Horatio Sparkins.—Mr. and Mrs.
Malderton. The Misses Malderton (Teresa and
Marianne). Frederick and Thomas Malderton.
Flamwell. Mr. Barton.

Chap. 6.—The Black Veil.—The Surgeon and his boy. His Visitor.

Chap. 7.—The Steam Excursion.—Mr. Percy Noakes, law student. Mrs. Stubbs, landlady. Mrs. Taunton. The Misses Emily and Sophia Taunton. Mr. Hardy. Mr. Loggins. Mr. Samuel Briggs. The Misses Briggs. The Fleetwoods. The Wakefields. Mr. Edkins. Mr. Wizzle. Mr. Alexander Briggs. Captain Helves. Mr. Simson.

Chap. 8.—The Great Winglebury Duel.—Alexander Trott, Esq. Horace Hunter. Emily Brown. Miss Julia Manners. Mr. Joseph Overton, mayor. Boots at the Lion. Lord Peter. Hon. Augustus Flair. Mrs. Williamson, landlady, Winglebury Arms.

Chap. 9.—Mrs. Joseph Porter.—Mr. and Mrs. Gattleton. Mr. Sempronius Gattleton. The Misses Gattleton. Mr. Evans. Mrs. Joseph Porter. Miss Emma Porter. Mr. Thomas Balderstone (Uncle Tom). Mr. Harleigh. Mr. Jenkins. Mr. Cape. Mr. Brown. The Smiths. The Gubbinses. The Nixons. The Dixons. The Hicksons. Sir Thomas Glumper.

Chap. 10.—A Passage in the Life of Mr. Watkins Tottle.

1st.—Mr. Tottle. Mr. and Mrs. Gabriel Parsons. Rev. Charles Timson. Miss Lillerton.

2nd.—Mr. Solomon Jacobs, sheriff's officer. Mr. Walker. Mr. Willis. Ikey.

Chap. 11.—The Bloomsbury Christening.—Mr. Nicodemus Dumps. Mr. Charles Kitterbell, his

nephew. Mrs. Jemima Kitterbell and child. Mr. Danton.

Chap. 12.—The Drunkard's Death.

THE PICKWICK PAPERS,

1836 to 1837.

Chap. 1.—Mr. Samuel Pickwick. **Tracy Tupman.** Augustus Snodgrass. Nathaniel Winkle. Joseph Smiggers. Mr. Blotton. **The Pickwick** Club.

Chap. 2.—Alfred Jingle. **Goswell Street.** Commodore, coach to Rochester. **The Bull Inn.** The Ball and guests. The Clubbers. Smithies. Bulders and Snipes. Doctor **Slammer.** **Mrs.** Budger. Lieutenant Tappleton. **Dr. Payne.**

Chap. 3.—Dismal Jemmy and the Stroller's tale.

Chap. 4.—The Wardle Family. **Mr. Wardle.** Aunt Rachel. Emily. Isabella. Joe, **the fat** boy. Mr. Trundle. Manor Farm. **Dingley** Dell.

Chap. 5.—Shiney William and hostlers.

Chap. 6.—Old Mrs. Wardle. **Mr. Miller.** The Clergyman and other guests. **Story of the Edmunds Family.**

Chap. 7.—Muggleton. **Messrs.** Luffey, Dumkins, Podder and Struggles, cricketers. **The Blue** Lion. Mr. Staple.

Chap. 10.—White Hart Inn, Borough. **Sam** Weller. Mr. Perker, lawyer to Mr. **Pickwick.**

Chap. 11.—Eatanswill.   The Leather Bottle, Cobham.   Bill Stumps.   The Madman's Manuscript.

Chap. 12.—Mrs. Bardell, Mr. Pickwick's landlady.   Master Bardell.

Chap. 13.—The Eatanswill Gazette.   Eatanswill Independent.   Buffs and Blues.   The Hon. Samuel Slumkey and Horatio Fizkin, Esq., Parliamentary candidates.   Mr. Pott, Editor of Eatanswill Gazette.   Mrs. Pott.   "The Peacock." "Town Arms."   The Mayor of Eatanswill.

Chap. 14.—The Bagman's Story.   Bilson and Slum.   Tom Smart.   Jinkins and the widow.

Chap. 15.—Mr. and Mrs. Leo Hunter.   Count Smorltork.   Mr. Solomon Lucas.   Mr. Charles FitzMarshall.

Chap. 16.—Job Trotter.   The Angel.   Bury St. Edmunds.   Miss Tomkins of Westgate House School.   Servants.   Pupils and Teachers.

Chap. 17.—The Parish Clerk.   Nathaniel Pipkin.   Old Lobbs.   Maria, his daughter.   Cousins Kate and Henry.

Chap. 18.—Goodwin, Mrs. Potts' maid.   Messrs. Dodson and Fogg, solicitors to Mrs. Bardell.

Chap. 19.—Martin, the tall gamekeeper.   Capt. Boldwig.   Hunt and Wilkins, gardeners.

Chap. 20.—Messrs. Wicks, Jackson and others, clerks to Dodson and Fogg.   Mr. Weller, senr. Mr. Lowten, Perkers' clerk.   The "Magpie and Stump."   Jack Bamber and others.

Chap. 21.—Stories of tenants of Clifford's Inn, and Heyling, his wife and child.

Chap. 22.—Mr. Peter Magnus. The Great White Horse, Ispwich.

Chap. 24.—Miss Witherfield (f.m. 22). George Nupkins, Esq., Mayor of Ipswich. Muzzle, his footman. Jinks, clerk. Grummer and Dubbley, constables.

Chap. 25.—Mrs. and Miss Nupkins. Mary (f. m. 23). Cook. The Porkenhams.

Chap. 26.—Mrs. Cluppins and Mrs. Sanders, friends of Mrs. Bardell. The George and Vulture, City.

Chap. 27.—Mrs. Weller, senr. Rev. Mr. Stiggins. The Marquis of Granby, Dorking.

Chap. 28.—Arabella Allen.

Chap. 29.—Gabriel Grub and the Goblins.

Chap. 30.—Benjamin Allen and Bob Sawyer.

Chap. 31.—Sergeant Snubbin and Mr Phunkey. Mr. Mallard, clerk to Snubbin.

Chap. 32.—Mr. and Mrs. Raddle, Bob Sawyer's landlord and landlady. Mr. Gunter. Mr. Noddy and Jack Hopkins, guests.

Chap. 33.—The Blue Boar, Leadenhall Market. "The Brick Lane Branch of the United Grand Junction Ebenezer Temperance Association." Mr. Anthony Humm. Mr. Jonas Mudge. Brother Tadger.

Chap. 34.—Sergeant Buzfuz and Mr. Skimpin. Mr. Justice Stareleigh and others.

Chap. 35.—Mr. and Mrs. Dowler. Angelo Cyrus Bantam. Dowager Lady Snuphanuph. Lord Mutanhed. Mr. Crushton. Mrs. Colonel Wugsby.

Miss Bolo.   Misses Matinter.   The White Hart Hotel, Bath.   The Assembly Rooms.

Chap. 36.--Mrs. Craddock.   Legend of Prince Bladud.

Chap. 37.—Mr. John Smauker (f.m. 35).   Mr. Tuckle (Blazes.)   Mr. Whiffers.   Footmen, etc.

Chap. 38.—The Bush at Bristol.   Nockemorf.

Chap. 39.—The surly groom.   The scientific gentleman and his servant, Pruffle.

Chap. 40.--Messrs. Smouch and Namby, Sheriff's officers.   The Fleet Prison.   Mr. Ayresleigh.   Mr. Price.   The lame man.   Crookey. Porkin and Snob.   Sniggle and Blink.   Stumpy and Deacon.

Chap. 41.—Mr. Tom Roker, turnkey.   Mr. Smangle.   Mr. Mivins.

Chap. 42.—Martin. The Chaplain. Mr. Simpson. Prisoners in Fleet.   The Chancery prisoner and others.   The Snuggery.

Chap. 43.—Mr. Solomon Pell, attorney.

Chap. 44.—The Cobbler, prisoner in Fleet.

Chap. 46.—Mrs. Rodgers, lodger to Mrs. Bardell. Isaac, officer.

Chap. 47.—Messrs. Snicks and Prosee, guests of Mr. Perker.

Chap. 48.—Arabella Allen's aunt (f.m. 38).   The one-eyed Bagman.   Martin (f.m. 39).

Chap. 49.—The Bagman's Uncle.   Jack Martin. Marquis of Filletoville.

Chap 50.—Mr. Winkle, sen.

Chap. 51.—" The Saracen's Head," Towcester. Mr. Slurk, editor of Eatanswill Independent.

Chap. 55.—Mr. Wilkins Flasher, stockbroker. Mr. Simmery.

OLIVER TWIST, 1837 to 1838.

Chap. 1.—Oliver.   His Mother.   Parish Surgeon.   The Workhouse.   Parish Nurse.

Chap. 2.—Mr. Bumble, beadle.   Mrs. Mann, the matron of branch workhouse.   Mr. Limbkins, Chairman of the Board.

Chap. 3.—Gamfield, chimney sweep.   Magistrates.

Chap. 4.—Mr. Sowerberry, parochial undertaker, Oliver's first master.   Mrs. Sowerberry.   Charlotte, the maid.

Chap. 5.—Noah Claypole, Sowerberry's assistant. The Pauper's funeral.

Chap. 7.—Dick, the workhouse child.

Chap. 8.—Jack Dawkins—the Artful Dodger. Fagin the Jew and his pupils.

Chap. 9.—Charley Bates.   Bet and Nancy.

Chap. 10.—Old Gentleman at bookstall—Mr. Brownlow.

Chap. 11.—Mr. Fang, magistrate.   The bookstall keeper.

Chap. 12.—Mrs. Bedwin, Mr. Brownlow's housekeeper.

Chap. 13.—Bill Sikes and his dog.

Chap. 14.—Mr. Grimwig, Mr. Brownlow's friend.

Chap. 15.—Barney the Jew.

Chap. 16.—Bull's Eye (f.m. 13).

Chap 18.—Tom Chitling, thief.

Chap. 19.—Toby Crackit, thief. Chertsey.

Chap. 23.—Mrs. Corney, matron of workhouse where Oliver was born. Mr. Grannett, overseer.

Chap. 24.—Two workhouse nurses, Anny and Martha. Apothecary's apprentice. Old Sally, Oliver's first nurse (f.m. 1).

Chap. 26.—Mr. Lively, the clothes-salesman of Field Lane. Landlord of the Three Cripples. Monks, Oliver's half brother. Phil Barker.

Chap. 27.—Mr Slout, Master of Workhouse.

Chap 28.—Brittles, lad of all work. Mr. Giles, steward to Mrs. Maylie. The travelling Tinker. The Cook and Housemaid.

Chap. 29.—Mrs. Maylie. Rose, her niece (adopted). Doctor Losberne.

Chap. 30.—The Constable. Bow Street Officers

Chap. 31.—Blathers and Duff. Conkey Chickweed and The Family Pet, thieves. Jem Spyers, officer.

Chap. 32.—The Humpbacked Man.

Chap. 34.—Harry Maylie, Mrs. Maylie's son.

Chap. 42.—Mr. and Mrs. Morris Bolter (alias Claypole).

Chap. 49.—Edward Leeford (alias Monks). His late father and mother.

Chap. 50.—Mr. Kags, returned transport.

Chap. 51.—Agnes Fleming (f.m. 1).

Chap. 52.—Fagin's jailers.

NICHOLAS NICKLEBY, 1838 to 1839.

Chap. 1.—Mr. Godfrey Nickleby and his wife.

His sons Ralph and Nicholas.   His uncle Ralph Nickleby.

Chap. 2.—Newman Noggs, clerk to Ralph Nickleby.   Office in Golden Square.   Mr. Bonney.   Sir Matthew Pupker, chairman to " United Metropolitan Improved Hot Muffin and Crumpet Baking and Punctual Delivery Company."

Chap. 3.—Mrs. Nickleby.   Kate and Nicholas, her children.   Miss La Creevy, portrait painter. Mr. Squeers.   Dotheboys Hall.   Saracen's Head, Snow Hill.

Chap. 4.—Snawley and his boys.   Belling, new boy.

Chap. 5.—Passengers by coach to Yorkshire.

Chap. 6.—Tales told by passengers.   " The Five Sisters of York."   " The Baron of Grogzwig." The George and New Inn.   Greta Bridge.

Chap. 7.—Mrs. Squeers.

Chap. 8.—Smike.   Bolder.   Cobbey.   Graymarsh and Mobbs, Squeers' pupils.

Chap. 9.—Fanny Squeers.   Matilda Price, her friend.   John Browdie.

Chap. 10.—Mr. and Madame Mantalini.   Miss Knag, forewoman to above.

Chap. 11.—Phœbe or Phib, Squeers' servant, (f.m. 7).

Chap. 13.—Tomkins, pupil of Squeers.

Chap. 14.—Mr. Crowl.   Mr. and Mrs. Kenwigs. Morleena Kenwigs and sisters.   Mr. Lillyvick, collector.   Mr. and Mrs. Cutler.   George.   Mr. Snewkes.   Miss Green.   Miss Petowker and others, guests at Kenwigs' party.

Chap. 16.—The General Agency Office and clients. The Fat Lady, proprietress. Tom, her clerk. Mr. Gregsbury, M.P., of Manchester Buildings. Mr. Pugstyles. Mr. Johnson, alias Nicholas.

Chap. 18.—Mr. Mortimer Knag. Mrs. Blockson, charwoman. Customers of Madame Mantalini.

Chap. 19.—Sir Mulberry Hawk. Lord Frederick Verisopht. Mr. Pluck. Mr. Pyke. Mr. Snobb. Colonel Chowser.

Chap. 21.—Mr. Scaley and Mr. Tix, brokers. Mr. and Mrs. Wititterly. Alphonse, page. Sir Tumley Snuffim, physician.

Chap. 22.—Mr. Vincent Crummles and boys.

Chap. 23.—Mrs. Crummles. The Indian Savage. Ninetta, or the Infant Phenomenon. Mr. Folair. Mr. and Mrs. Lenville. Miss Ledbrook. Miss Snevellicci. Miss Bravassa. Miss Belvawney. Miss Gazings. Mrs. Grudden—stage company. Bulph, pilot.

Chap. 24.— Mr. and Mrs. Curdle. Mrs. Borum and family.

Chap. 30.—Mr. and Mrs. Snevellicci.

Chap. 35.—Brothers Ned and Charles Cheeryble. Tim Linkinwater. Mr. Trimmers.

Chap. 36.—Mr. Lumbey, doctor.

Chap. 37.—Tim Linkinwater's sister. David, butler to Brothers Cheeryble. Bank Clerk.

Chap. 40.—Cecilia Bobster.

Chap. 41.—The Mad Gentleman (f.m. 37).

Chap. 43.—Frank Cheeryble, nephew to Brothers Cheeryble.

Chap. 44.—Brooker.

Chap. 46.—Mr. Bray.   Madeline Bray and servant (f.m. 16).

Chap. 47.—Arthur Gride, miser.

Chap. 48.—Mr. Snittle Timberry.   The African Knife Swallower.

Chap. 51.—Peg Sliderskew, Arthur Gride's housekeeper.

MASTER HUMPHREY'S CLOCK, 1840 to 1841.

Chap. 1.—Master Humphrey.   His Barber.   The Clock.   The Deaf Gentleman.   The Lord Mayor, Joe Toddyhigh.   Gog and Magog Chronicles. The Bowyer.   Mistress Alice.   Hugh Graham.

Chap. 2.—Jack Redburn.   Mr. Owen Miles. Belinda.

Chap. 3.—Mr. Pickwick and the Wellers.   Father Son and Grandson.   John Podgers.   Will Marks. The Mask.

Chap. 5.—Mr. Slithers (f.m. 1).   Jinkinson.

Chap. 6.—Miss Benton (f.m. 1).

THE OLD CURIOSITY SHOP, 1840.

Chap. 1.—Little Nell and her grandfather.   Kit, assistant to grandfather.

Chap. 2.—Fred Trent, Nell's brother.   Dick Swiveller.

Chap. 3.—Daniel Quilp, money lender, etc., and Mrs. Quilp, of Tower Hill.

Chap. 4.—Mrs. Jiniwin, Quilp's mother-in-law. Mrs. George and Mrs. Simmons, friends of above.

Chap. 5.—Quilp's boy.

Chap. 7.—Sophia Wackles, Dick's sweetheart.

Chap. 8.—Mrs. Wackles.   Misses Melissa and Jane Wackles.   Mr. Cheggs, market gardener. Miss Cheggs.

Chap. 10.—Mrs. Nubbles (Kit's mother) and children.

Chap. 11.—Sampson Brass, lawyer, of Bevis Marks.

Chap. 13.—Little Jacob (f.m. 10.)   The Glorious Apollers.

Chap. 14.—Mr. and Mrs. Garland and son, Abel. Mr. Witherden, notary.   Chuckster, clerk to Mr. Witherden.   Whisker, Mr. Garland's pony.

Chap. 15.—Cottager's family where Nell and Grandfather rest on their journey.

Chap 16.—Thomas Codlin and Short (Harris.) Punch's showmen.

Chap. 17.—Grinder, stilt-walker.

Chap. 18.—Landlord of The Jolly Sandboys. Jerry, manager of the dancing dogs.

Chap. 19.—Mr. Vuffin and Sweet William, proprietors of giant and conjurers.

Chap. 22.—Barbara, Mrs. Garland's servant.

Chap. 24.—The Schoolmaster of the village.

Chap. 25.—Little Harry, the sick pupil.

Chap. 26.—Mrs. Jarley, waxwork proprietress. George, carter and driver of caravan.

Chap. 28.—Mr. Slum, poetic advertiser.

Chap. 29.—James Groves, landlord of the " Valiant Soldier."   Isaac List and gruff companion, cardplayers.   Luke Withers.   Miss Montflathers, school mistress.

Chap. 31.—Miss Edwards, pupil teacher.

Chap. 33.—Miss Sally Brass.

Chap. 34.—The single gentleman, lodger at the Brasses. The small servant.

Chap. 36.—Old Foxey, the Brasses father. The Marchioness.

Chap. 39.—Barbara's mother.

Chap. 41.—Little Bethel and preacher.

Chap. 42.—Jowl (f.m. 29.)

Chap. 43.—The Boatmen.

Chap. 44.—The Ironworker.

Chap. 50.—Tom Scott (f.m. 5.)

Chap. 52.—The Clergyman and his friend the Bachelor, Mr. Garland's brother. Marton, the schoolmaster (f.m. 22.)

Chap. 53.—The Sexton.

Chap. 54.—David, the sexton's friend and assistant.

BARNABY RUDGE, 1841.

Chap. 1.—The Maypole Inn, Chigwell. John Willet, landlord. Tom Cobb, chandler and post office keeper. Phil Parkes, ranger. Solomon Daisy, parish clerk. The stranger, Edward Chester. Joe Willet, landlord's son. Mr. Geoffrey Haredale, of the Warren. His niece, Emma. The late Mr. Reuben Haredale, brother to Geoffrey. Rudge, his steward.

Chap. 2.—Gabriel Varden, locksmith.

Chap. 3.—Mrs. Varden and Dolly Varden. Barnaby Rudge, the idiot.

Chap. 4.—Simon Tappertit, apprentice to Gabriel Varden. Mrs. Rudge.

3

Chap. 6.—Grip, the Raven.

Chap. 7.—Miss Miggs, Mrs. Varden's servant.

Chap. 8.—Stagg, the blind man.   The Prentice Knights.   Mark Gilbert.   Thomas Curson, his master.

Chap. 10.—Hugh, of the Maypole.   Mr. Chester.

Chap. 23.—Peak, servant to Mr. Chester.

Chap. 31.—The Recruiting Sergeant.

Chap. 35.—Lord George Gordon.   Gashford, his secretary.   John Grueby, servant.

Chap. 36.—Dennis, the Hangman.

Chap. 47.—The Country Justice of the Peace and his wife.

Chap. 49.—General Conway.   Colonel Gordon. Magistrate.   Horse Guards.

Chap. 58.—Tom Green.   The sergeant.   Sir John Fielding.

Chap. 61.—The Lord Mayor.   Mr. Langdale, vintner of Holborn.

Chap. 64.—Mr. Akerman, head gaoler of New-gate.

Chap. 66.—Lord and Lady Mansfield.

Chap. 67.—Lord President.   Lord Rockingham. Lord Algernon Percy.

Chap. 73.—Lord Saville.   Mr. Herbert.

AMERICAN NOTES, 1842.

Chaps. 1 and 2.—The Voyage Out.   The Britannia.

Chap. 3.—Boston.   Public Buildings.   Asylum for the Blind.   Laura Bridgeman.   Dr. Howe. Mr. Hart, master.   Oliver Caswell.   Hospital for

Insane. Inmates and Physician. School and House of Reformation. House of Correction. Mr. Taylor. Theatres.

Chap. 4.—American railroads. The Mills. Lowell.

Chap. 5.—Worcester. Hartford. Insane Asylum. Doctor and Inmates. Deaf and Dumb Asylum. New Haven Steamboats.

Chap. 6.—New York. Prisons. The Tombs and Public Institutions.

Chap. 7.—Philadelphia. Eastern Penitentiary and Inmates. Other Institutions.

Chap. 8.—Baltimore. Washington. House of Representatives. White House and other buildings. The President.

Chap. 9.—The River steamboats. Stage coaches, drivers and passengers. Richmond. Harrisburg Mail. Canal boats.

Chap. 10.—Canal boat arrangements. Pittsburgh.

Chap. 11.—The Messenger steamboat. Emigrants. Cincinnati.

Chap. 12.—The Pike steamboat. Pitchlynn. Indian chief, Choctaw Tribe. Louisville. The Kentucky Giant, Porter. Mississippi river. St. Louis. Fulton steamboat. Buildings of St. Louis.

Chap. 13.—The Looking Glass Prairie. Belleville. Dr. Crocus, phrenologist.

Chap. 14.—Stage Coach to Columbus. Sandusky. Niagara.

Chap. 15.—Table Rock.   Queenston.   Toronto. Montreal.   Quebec.   Lake boats.   Shaker village.

Chap. 16.—Voyage home and passengers.

Chap. 17.—Slavery.

Chap. 18.—American characteristics.

MARTIN CHUZZLEWIT, 1843 to 1844.

Chap. 1.—Earliest Chuzzlewits, Diggory, Toby, etc.

Chap. 2.—Salisbury.   The Blue Dragon.   Mr. Pecksniff.   Charity and Mercy Pecksniff.   Tom Pinch.   John Westlock.

Chap. 3.—Mrs. Lupin.   Old Martin Chuzzlewit.   Mary Graham.

Chap. 4.—Montague Tigg.   Chevy Slyme.   Mr. and Mrs. Spottletoe.   Anthony and Jonas Chuzzlewit.   George Chuzzlewit.   Mrs. Ned Chuzzlewit, the strong-minded lady, and three daughters ; a cousin, grandnephew and others.

Chap. 5.—Mark Tapley.   Martin Chuzzlewit.

Chap. 8.—Mrs. Todgers and her boarding house.

Chap. 9.—Ruth Pinch and pupil (The Seraph.) The Brass and Copper Founder.   Bailey, boy at Todgers (f.m. 8.)   Mr. Jinkins (f.m. 8.)   Mr. Gander. The youngest gentleman, and other boarders.

Chap. 11.—Old Chuffey.

Chap. 13.—Bill Simmons, van driver.   Lummy Ned, guard of light Salisbury coach.   David, pawnbroker.

Chap. 15.—The Screw Packet and passengers.

Chap. 16.—New York Newspaper Boys.   " The Sewer," " The Stabber," " Private Listener," " Family Spy," " Peeper ," " Plunderer," " Keyhole Reporter," " Rowdy Journal." Colonel Diver, editor of "New York Rowdy Journal." Jefferson Brick, war correspondent. Major Pawkins, boarding house proprietor. Mrs. Pawkins. Mrs. Jefferson Brick. Professor Mullit, and other boarders.

Chap. 17.—Cicero, the negro. Mr. Bevan. Mr. and Mrs. Norris and family. General Fladdock.

Chap. 19.—Mrs. Sairey Gamp. Mr. Mould, undertaker. Tacker, Mould's assistant. Mrs. Harris.

Chap. 21.—Mr. La Fayette Kettle. General Choke. Mr. Scadder, agent. Meeting of the Watertoast Sympathisers. The Watertoast Gazette.

Chap. 22.—Captain Kedgick. Mrs. Hominy. The Modern Gracchi. Mr. Putnam Smiff.

Chap. 23.—New Thermopylae. Eden.

Chap. 25.—Mrs. Mould. The two Misses Mould. Betsy Prig. The Bull Inn, Holborn. Landlord and landlady. The Patient.

Chap. 26.—Poll or Paul Sweedlepipe, bird fancier and barber (f.m. 19.)

Chap. 27.—The Anglo-Bengalee Disinterested Loan and Life Insurance Company. David Crimple (f.m. 13), director. Bullamy, porter. Jobling, doctor. Nadgett.

Chap. 28.—Mr. Wolf and Mr. Pip, guests at dinner.

Chap. 29.—Mr. Lewsome (f.m. 25.)

Chap. 32.—Augustus Moddle (f.m. 9.)
Chap. 33.—Hannibal Chollop.
Chap. 34.—Hon. Elijah Pogram, member of congress.   Mr. Izzard.   Dr. Ginery Dunkle.   Mr. Jodd.   Julius Washington Merryweather Bib. Colonel Groper.   Professor Piper and Oscar Buffum, boarders at the National Hotel.   Miss Toppet and Miss Codger, two literary ladies.
Chap. 37.—Man in the Monument.
Chap. 39.—Mr. Fips.

PICTURES FROM ITALY, 1846.

The French Courier.   Landlord and lady of the Hôtel de l' Ecu d' Or.   The Sacristan.   Goblin of Avignon.   Antonio, cowman.   Theatres of Genoa. The Frenchman and Cappuccino Friar, on Nice boat.   The Old Priest.   Young Jesuit and Tuscan. Avvocáto and other passengers by coach from Genoa. Piacenza.   Parma Modena.   Peasants.   Bologna Cemetery.   The little Cicerone.   Ferrara.   Postillion, and various people met with.   Venice. Verona.   Mantua.   The Cicerone.   Milan. Switzerland.   Spezzia.   Carrara.   Pisa.   Siena to Rome.   Mass at St. Peter's.   The Carnival. Mr. and Mrs. Davis and party.   The Bambino of the Church of Ara Coeli.   St. Stefans Rotondo. Mamertine prisons.   Churches of St. Giovanni and St. Paolo.   San Sebastiano Catacombs.   An execution.   The Vatican.   Picture Galleries.   Suburbs of Rome.   Holy Week.   The Pope and thirteen men.   Pilgrims' supper.   Holy staircase.   Naples.

Herculaneum and Pompeii. Vesuvius. Mr. Pickle of Portici. Guides. The Hermitage. San Carlo. Lotteries. Monastery of Monte Cassino. The Raven. Inn at Valmontone. Florence. The Palaces and bridges. Cathedrals. Churches and Museum of Natural History. Places of interest and homeward route.

DOMBEY AND SON, 1847 to 1848.

Chap. 1.—Mr. and Mrs. Dombey. Florence and Paul Dombey. Miss Tox. Mrs. Chick, Louisa, sister to Mr. Dombey. Dr. Parker Peps. Mr. Pilkins, doctor. Mrs. Blockitt, nurse.

Chap. 2.—Mr. Chick. Mr. Toodles. Mrs. Polly Toodles, alias Richards, Paul's nurse. Toodles' children. Jemima, Mrs. Toodles' sister. Biler Toodles, or Rob the Grinder.

Chap. 3.—Susan Nipper, Spitfire.

Chap. 4.—Solomon Gills, ships' instrument maker. Walter Gay, his nephew. Captain Cuttle. Mr. Carker, manager in Dombey's office. Mr. Morfin.

Chap. 5.—Towlinson, Dombey's footman.

Chap. 6 .—"Good Mrs. Brown." Staggs' Gardens. Mr. Clark. Mr. Carker, jun., Dombey's clerk.

Chap. 7.—Princess's Place. Major Bagstock. The Native, his servant.

Chap. 8.—Mrs. Wickham, Paul's second nurse. Mrs. Pipchin, children's boarding house keeper. Berinthia, or Berry, her niece. Master Bitherstone and Miss Pankey, boarders.

Chap. 9.—Brig Place.   Mrs. Macstinger.   Mr. Brogley, broker.

Chap. 11.—Dr. Blimber.   Mrs. Blimber.   Cornelia Blimber.   Mr. Feeder, B.A., usher.   Mr. Toots.

Chap. 12.—Briggs, Johnson and Tozer, pupils. Old Glubb.   Melia, servant.

Chap. 13.—Perch, messenger at Dombey's office. Mrs. Perch.

Chap. 14.—The Apothecary.   The Workman. Sir Barnet Skettles.   Lady Skettles.   Master Skettles.   Mr. Baps, dancing master.   Mrs. Baps. Diogenes, Toots' dog.

Chap. 15.—Rev. Melchisedeck Howler.   Captain Bunsby.

Chap. 21.—Mrs. Skewton, Cleopatra.   Mrs. Granger (Edith), her daughter.   Withers, page. Cousin Feenix.

Chap. 22.—Harriet Carker.   The Game Chicken. The Black Badger.

Chap. 23.—Alexander Macstinger.   The Cautious Clara, Bunsby's ship.

Chap. 24.—Kate, the orphan, and her Aunt. Martha, the cripple, and her Father.

Chap. 25.—Juliana Macstinger.

Chap. 31.—Mrs. Miff, pew-opener. Mr. Sowndes, beadle (f.m. 5.)

Chap. 34.—Alice Marwood, daughter of "Good Mrs. Brown."

Chap. 36.—Guests at Dombey's dinner party. Flowers, Mrs. Skewton's maid (f.m. 27).

Chap. 60.—Mrs. Bokem—friend of Mrs. Macstinger.

DAVID COPPERFIELD, 1849 to 1850.

Chap. 1.—Mr. Copperfield.   Mrs. Clara Copperfield.   Mr. Chillip, doctor.   Betsy Trotwood, aunt. Peggotty, Mrs. Copperfield's servant.   Ham Peggotty, her nephew.   Blunderstone Rookery.

Chap. 2.—Mr. Murdstone.   Brooks of Sheffield. Mr. Pasnidge.   Mr. Quinion.   Mrs. Grayper.

Chap. 3.—Mr. Peggotty, Dan.   Mrs. Gummidge. Little Emily.   The "Willing Mind."

Chap. 4.—Miss Murdstone.

Chap. 5.—Mr. Barkis, carrier (f.m. 3.)   Waiter at Yarmouth.   Mrs. Fibbitson.   Salem House School.   Mr. Mell, usher.   Mr., Mrs. and Miss Creakle, principals of Salem House School.

Chap. 6.—James Steerforth.   Tommy Traddles, pupils.   Tungay, man with wooden leg (f.m. 5.) Mr. Sharp, first master.

Chap. 9.—Mr. Omer, funeral furnisher.   Minnie, his daughter.   Joram, assistant.

Chap. 10.—Murdstone and Grinby.

Chap. 11.—Mick Walker, warehouse boy at Murdstone and Grinby's.   Mr. and Mrs. Micawber. Wilkins and Emma Micawber.   Clickett, the " Orfling " servant.   " Mealy Potatoes."   Gregory. Tipp.   Captain Hopkins.

Chap. 12.—The long-legged young man and donkey cart.

Chap. 13.—Mr. Dolloby, keeper of second-hand clothes shop.   The " ugly old man," ditto.   Janet, servant to Betsy Trotwood.   Mr. Dick (Mr. Richard Babley), boarder, etc.

Chap. 15.—Mr. Wickfield, lawyer.   Agnes Wickfield.   Uriah Heep, clerk.

Chap. 16.—Dr. Strong, schoolmaster.   Mrs. Strong, his wife Annie.   Jack Maldon, Annie's cousin.   Mrs. Markleham, Annie's mother, the Old Soldier.   Adams, pupil of Dr. Strong.

Chap. 17.—Mrs. Heep (f.m. 16), Uriah's mother.

Chap. 18.—The Misses Nettingalls' establishment.   Miss Shepherd, pupil.   The Eldest Miss Larkins.   Mr. Larkins.   Mr. Chestle.   Capt. Bailey.

Chap. 19.—Waiter at the Golden Cross.   William, driver of Canterbury coach .

Chap. 20.—Daisy (David).   Mrs. Steerforth. Rosa Dartle.

Chap. 21.—Littimer, Steerforth's servant.

Chap 22.—Miss Mowcher, the dwarf.   Martha Endell.

Chap. 23.—Spenlow and Jorkins, proctors.   Mrs. Crupp, lodging house keeper.

Chap. 24.—Grainger and Markham, Steerforth's friends.

Chap. 25.—Mr. and Mrs. Waterbrook.   Mr. and Mrs. Henry Spiker, Hamlet's aunt.   Mr. and Mrs. Gulpidge, guests at Mr. Waterbrook's.

Chap. 26.—Tiffey, Mr. Spenlow's clerk.   Dora Spenlow.   " Jip," Dora's dog.

Chap. 33.—Julia Mills and Mr. Mills, her father. Red Whisker.

Chap. 34.—Sophy and Sarah Crewler.

Chap. 41.—Misses Spenlow, Lavinia and Clarissa, Dora's aunts (f.m. 38.)   Rev. Horace Crewler and Mrs. Crewler.   Mr. Pidger.

Chap. 47.—Betsy Trotwood's husband (f.m. 17.)

Chap. 59.—Miss Crewler, Louisa Margaret and Lucy.

BLEAK HOUSE, 1852 to 1853.

Chap 1.—The Lord High Chancellor. Jarndyce and Jarndyce. Tom Jarndyce. The little mad woman. The man from Shropshire. Mr. Tangle, counsel. The Two Wards in Chancery.

Chap. 2.—Sir Leicester Dedlock. Lady Dedlock. Hon. Bob Stables. Mr. Tulkinghorn, lawyer.

Chap. 3.—Esther Summerson. Miss Barbary, her aunt and godmother. Mrs. Rachel, her servant. Messrs. Kenge and Carboy, Solicitors. Gentleman in coach. Miss Flite (f.m. 1.) Miss Donny. Ada Clare and Richard Carstone (f.m. 1.) John Jarndyce.

Chap. 4.—Mr. and Mrs. Jellyby. Caddy and Peepy Jellyby. Borrioboola-Gha. Mr. Quale, philanthropist. Mr. Guppy, clerk to Kenge and Carboy. Thavies Inn

Chap. 5.—Krook, rag and bone dealer. Lady Jane, his cat. Nemo, his lodger, law writer.

Chap. 6.—Mr. Harold Skimpole. Coavinses.

Chap. 7.—Chesney Wold, Leicestershire, Sir L. Dedlock's country house. Mrs. Rouncewell, house-keeper; her sons George and the ironmaster, her grandson Watt. Rosa, maid. Sir Morbury Dedlock and Lady.

Chap. 8.—Mrs. Pardiggle.   Her sons Egbert, Oswald, Francis, Felix, and Alfred.   Mr. O. A. Pardiggle.   Mr. Gusher.   The brickmaker and family.   Jenny, his wife.

Chap. 9.—Mr. Laurence Boythorn.

Chap. 10.—Mr. Snagsby, law stationer.   Mrs. Snagsby.   Guster, servant.   Two prentices.   Peffer, Snagsby's   predecessor.   Cook's Court, Cursitor Street.

Chap. 11.—The young surgeon.   The beadle. The coroner.   Mrs. Perkins and Mrs. Anastatia Piper, Krook's neighbours.   Little Swills, comic vocalist.   Landlord of the Sols Arms.   Jo, crossing sweeper.

Chap. 12.—Mlle. Hortense.   Lord Boodle and his retinue.   Right Honorable William Buffy and his retinue.

Chap. 13.—Mr. Bayham Badger, doctor.   Mrs. B. Badger.   Captain Swosser and Professor Dingo, Mrs. Badger's former husbands.

Chap. 14.—Mr. Turveydrop and his son Prince. Dancing Academy, Newman Street.   Allan Woodcourt (f.m. 11.)

Chap. 15.—Neckitt, sheriff's officer.   Mrs. Blinder.   Gridley (f.m. 1.)   Charley, Emma, and Tom Neckitt.

Chap. 17.—Mrs. Woodcourt, Allan's mother.

Chap. 19.—Mr. and Mrs. Chadband.

Chap. 20.—Young Smallweed, Bart.   Weevle, alias Jobling (f.m. 7.)

Chap. 21.—Grandfather and Grandmother Smallweed.   Judy Smallweed, Bart's sister.   Mr. George,

the trooper (f.m. 7.)   Phil, George's man at the shooting gallery.

Chap. 22.—Mr. Buckett, detective.

Chap. 26.—Captain Hawdon.

Chap. 27.—Mr. Matthew Bagnet. Mrs. Bagnet. Quebec, Malta, and Woolwich Bagnet.

Chap. 28.—Volumnia Dedlock, cousin to Sir Leicester.

Chap. 30.—Miss Wisk.

Chap. 31.—Liz, the brickmaker's wife.

Chap. 32.—Miss Melvilleson, vocalist at Sols Arms.

Chap. 33.—Bogsby, landlord (f.m. 11.)

Chap. 37.—W. Grubble, landlord of the Dedlock Arms.   Mr. Vholes, lawyer, and his three daughters, Emma, Jane, and Caroline.

Chap. 38.—Mrs. Guppy (f.m. 9.)

Chap. 40.—Cousins of Sir Leicester Dedlock.

Chap. 43.—Mrs. Skimpole and three daughters, Arethusa, Laura, and Kitty.

Chap. 53.—Mrs. Buckett.

HARD TIMES, 1854..

BOOK THE FIRST

Chaps. 1 and 2.—Thomas Gradgrind.   Mr. M'Choakumchild, schoolmaster.   Government officer.   Sissy Jupe and Bitzer, scholars.

Chap. 3.—Coketown.   Signor Jupe.   Merrylegs, his dog.   Josephine Sleary.   Louisa and Thomas Gradgrind.   Stone Lodge.

Chap. 4.—Mr. Josiah Bounderby.   Adam Smith, Malthus and Jane Gradgrind.   Mrs. Gradgrind.

Chap 6.—Pegasus's Arms.   Mr. Sleary, circus master.   Mr. E. W. B. Childers and Master Kidderminster, performers.

Chap. 7.—Mrs. Sparsit, Mr. Bounderby's housekeeper.   Lady Scadgers, Mrs. Sparsit's great aunt.

Chap. 9.—Mrs. M'Choakumchild.

Chap. 10.—Stephen Blackpool, weaver.   Rachel. Stephen's wife.

Chap. 12.—Mr. Josiah Bounderby's mother.

BOOK THE SECOND

Chap. 2.—Mr. James Harthouse (f.m. 1.)
Chap. 4.—Slackbridge.
Chap. 6.—Mrs. Pegler (f.m. 12, Book 1.)

LITTLE DORRIT, 1855 to 1856.

BOOK THE FIRST

Chap. 1.—Marseilles.   The Prison.   John Baptist Cavalletto.   Monsr. Rigaud.   The gaoler and his child.   Monsr. and Madame Barronneau.

Chap. 2.—Mr. and Mrs. Meagles.   Pet, or Minnie Meagles.   Tattycoram.   Arthur Clennam. Miss Wade.

Chap. 3.—Mrs. Clennam. Jeremiah Flintwinch. Affery Flintwinch.

Chap. 4.—Double,

Chap. 5.—Little Dorrit, Amy (f.m. 3.)

Chap. 6.—The Marshalsea Prison. Mr. William Dorrit, father of the Marshalsea. The Plasterer. Bob, the Turnkey. Dr. Haggage. Mrs. Bangham.

Chap. 7.—Edward (Tip) and Fanny Dorrit. The Dancing Master. The Milliner.

Chap. 8.—Frederick Dorrit (f.m. 7.) The Snuggery.

Chap. 9.—Mr. Cripples' Academy. Mr. Plornish (f.m. 6.) Bleeding Heart Yard. Maggy. Mr. Tite Barnacle.

Chap. 10.—The Circumlocution Office. The Barnacle family. Barnacle jun. The Stiltstalkings. Mews Street, Grosvenor Square. Mr. Wobbler. Mr. Daniel Doyce.

Chap. 11.—The Break of Day Chalons. Landlord, landlady, and guests. Monsr. Lagnier.

Chap. 12.—Mrs. Plornish. Mr. Christopher Casby. Mr. Pancks. Captain Maroon.

Chap. 13.—Flora Casby, Mrs. Finching. The Patriarch. Lord Decimus Tite Barnacle. Mr. F.'s Aunt.

Chap. 14.—The Sexton or Verger.

Chap. 16.—Twickenham. Mrs. Tickit, housekeeper.

Chap. 17.—Henry Gowan. Lion, his dog. Lady Jemima Bilbery. Lady Seraphina. Hon. Clementina Toozellem.

Chap. 18.—Mr. and Mrs. Chivery and young John, turnkey.

Chap. 20.—Society. Mrs. Merdle. Her parrot. Harley Street, Cavendish Square.

Chap. 21.—Mr. Merdle. Edmund Sparkler. Magnates at Merdle's dinner party. Bishop. Treasury. Horse Guards. Bar. Brother Bellows. Admiralty. Physician. The Chief Butler.

Chap. 25.—Mr. and Miss Rugg, Anastatia.

Chap. 26.—Hampton Court. Mrs. Gowan (f.m. 17.) Lord Lancaster Stiltstalking. Old Lady. Other Barnacles.

Chap. 30.—Blandois of Paris.

Chap. 31.—Old Nandy, Mrs. Plornish's father.

Chap. 34.—Other Barnacles.

Chap. 36.—The Marshal. Messrs. Peddle and Pool, solicitors.

BOOK THE SECOND

Chap. 1.—The Convent of the Great St. Bernard. The Young Father at Convent. Mrs. General.

Chap. 3.—Hotel at Martigny. Innkeeper.

Chap. 5.—Mr. Tinkler, valet to Mr. Dorrit. Mr. Eustace, the traveller.

Chap. 12.—Ferdinand Barnacle (f.m. 10, Book 1.)

Chap. 21.—Charlotte Dawes.

A TALE OF TWO CITIES, 1859.

BOOK THE FIRST

Chap. 2.—The Dover Mail. Joe, the guard. Tom, the coachman. Mr. Jarvis Lorry, passenger. Jerry. Tellson's Bank. "Mam'selle."

Chap. 4.—The Concord Bedchamber. Royal George, Dover. Miss Manette (f.m. 2.)

Chap. 5.—St. Antoine. Monsieur and Madame Defarge. Doctor Manette. Jacques. Gaspard.

BOOK THE SECOND

Chap. 1.—Mr. Cruncher, Jerry (f.m. 2, Book 1.) Mrs. Cruncher and young Jerry.

Chap. 2.—Charles Darnay. The Old Bailey. The Judge. Attorney General, etc.

Chap. 3—Solicitor General. John Barsad. Roger Cly. Mr. Stryver. Sidney Carton.

Chap. 6.—Miss Pross and her brother Solomon.

Chap. 7.—Monsigneur. The Farmer General. Monsieur the Marquis.

Chap. 8.—The mender of roads. Monsieur Gabelle. The villagers.

Chap. 15.—Damiens.

Chap. 21.—Little Lucie. Mrs. Stryver.

Chap. 22.—The Vengeance. Foulon.

Chap. 24.—St. Evremonde. Prison of Abbaye.

BOOK THE THIRD

Chap. 1.—La Guillotine. Prison of La Force.

Chap. 5.—The Woodsawyer. Carmagnole.

Chap. 6.—The Conciergerie and President.

Chap. 8.—The Good Republican, Brutus of Antiquity.

Chap. 9.—Samson.

Chap. 13.—The Little Seamstress.

4

GREAT EXPECTATIONS, 1860 to 1861.

Chap. 1.—Phillip Pirrip, Pip.   Joe Gargery, blacksmith.   The Convicts.   Mrs. Joe Gargery, sister to Pip.

Chap. 4.—Mr. and Mrs. Hubble.   Mr. Wopsle, clerk.   Uncle Pumblechook.

Chap 5.—The Sergeant and soldiers.

Chap. 7.—Mr. Wopsle's great-aunt.   Biddy, her great-granddaughter.

Chap. 8.—Miss Havisham of Satis House (f.m. 7.) Estella.

Chap. 10.—The Three Jolly Bargemen.   The strange man.

Chap. 11.—Camilla.   Cousin Raymond.   Sarah Pocket.   Matthew Pocket.   Georgiana.

Chap. 15.—Dolge Orlick.

Chap. 18.—Mr. Jaggers (f.m. 11.)

Chap. 19.—Mr. Trabb, tailor.   Trabb's boy.

Chap. 20.—Wemmick, clerk to Jaggers.

Chap. 21.—Herbert Pocket (f.m. 18.)

Chap. 22.—Handel, Pip.   Mrs. Pocket.   Alex and Jane Pocket.   Flopson and Millers, nurse-maids.

Chap. 23.—Bentley Drummle and Startop.   Mrs. Coiler.

Chap. 25.—The Aged Parent, Wemmick's father.

Chap. 26.—Mr. Jaggers' housekeeper.

Chap. 27.—Pepper or Avenger, Pip's boy.

Chap. 34.—The Finches of the Grove.

Chap. 37.—Miss Skiffins.   Clarriker.

Chap. 38.—Mrs. Brandley and her daughter.

Chap. 40.—Magwitch or Provis (f.m. 1.)

Chap. 42.—Compeyson (f.m. 1.)   Arthur Havisham.

Chap. 46.—Mrs. Whimple, lodging house keeper, (f.m. 22.)   Old Barley and his daughter Clara.

THE UNCOMMERCIAL TRAVELLER, 1860.

Chap. 1.—His General Line of Business.

Chap. 2.—The Shipwreck.—Wreck of the Royal Charter.   The two Welsh Clergymen,—Rev. Stephen Roose Hughes and Rev. Hugh Robert Hughes.   Llanallgo.

Chap. 3.—Wapping Workhouse.—Mr. Baker. Refractories and Oakum Head.

Chap. 4.—Two Views of a Cheap Theatre.— The Britannia Theatre, Hoxton.   The Pantomime and Drama.   The Preaching.

Chap. 5.—Poor Mercantile Jack.—Mr. Superintendent Sharpeye.   Trampfoot, Quickear, etc., policemen.

Chap. 6.—Refreshments for Travellers.—Station rooms.   Mr. and Mrs. Bogles.   Mr. and Mrs. Grazinglands.   Jarrings Hotel, etc.

Chap. 7.—Travelling Abroad.—The queer small boy.   Louis, servant.   Paris.   The Morgue. Strasburg.   Straudenheim.

Chap. 8.—The Great Tasmania's Cargo.—The discharged soldiers from India.   Pangloss.   Liverpool Workhouse.

Chap. 9.—City of London Churches.—Boanerges Boiler.

Chap. 10.—Shy Neighbourhoods.

Chap. 11.—Tramps.

Chap. 12.—Dulborough Town.—Timpson's, the coach office. Pickford's. Boles and Coles. The Theatre. Mechanics' Institutes. Mr. and Mrs. Joe Specks and family. The greengrocer.

Chap. 13.—Night Walks.—London Streets.

Chap. 14.—Chambers.—Mrs. Sweeney. Parkle. Mrs. Miggot. Parkle's fellow lodger. Mr. Testator. His visitor and others.

Chap. 15.—Nurse's Stories.—Captain Murderer and his wives. Chips, etc.

Chap. 16.—Arcadian London.—The Hatter. Mr., Mrs. and Miss Klem. The Doctor's servant of Saville Row. The Dentist's servant.

Chap. 17.—The Calais Night Mail.—Mr. and **Mrs.** Birmingham, of the Lord Warden Hotel, Dover. Passengers.

Chap. 18.—Some Recollections of Mortality.— The Morgue. Coroner's Jury.

Chap 19.—Birthday Celebrations.—Olympia Squires. Globson. Flipfield and family. Long-lost. Mayday.

Chap. 20.—Bound for the Great Salt Lake.— The Amazon Ship. Mormon Agent. Passengers. The Jobsons. Cleverleys. Dibbles, etc.

Chap. 21.—The City of the Absent.—Saint Ghastly Grim. The old man and woman making hay. Joseph and Celia, charity children. Garraways. Banks.

Chap. 22.—An Old Stage Coaching House.—The Dolphin's Head. J. Mellows. The Waitress.

The Coachmaker.   The Turnpike Keeper.   The Stonebreaker.

*Chap. 23.—The Boiled Beef of New England.—*Cooking Depots.

*Chap. 24.—Chatham Dockyard.—*The Spirit of the Fort.

*Chap. 25.—In the French-Flemish Country.—*Monsr. P. Salcy and family, dramatic artists.   The Fair.   Ventriloquist and Face-maker, etc.

*Chap. 26.—Medicine-Men of Civilisation.—*Sally Flanders and her husband's funeral.   Mr. Kindheart.

*Chap. 27.—Titbull's Almshouses.—*Mr. Battens. Mrs. Saggers.   Mrs. Quinch.   Mrs. Mitts.   The Greenwich pensioner.   The Chelsea pensioner.

*Chap. 28.—The Italian Prisoner.—*Giovanni Carlavero.   The Englishman.   The Advocate.   The Bottle of Wine.

1868-9.

Chap. 29.—The Short-Timers.

*Chap. 30.—A Small Star in the East.—*The Irishwoman and family.   The Boilermaker and others.

*Chap. 31.—Aboard Ship.—*Captain Cook and passengers.

*Chap. 32.—A Little Dinner in an Hour.—*Bullfinch.   Namelesston.   The Temeraire.   Mr. Indignation Cocker.

Chap. 33.—Mr. Barlow.

Chap. 34.—On an Amateur Beat.

Chap. 35.—A Plea for Total Abstinence.

Chap. 36.—The Ruffian.

OUR MUTUAL FRIEND, 1864 to 1865.

BOOK THE FIRST.

Chap. 1.—Gaffer Hexam.   Lizzie, his daughter.
Chap. 2.—Mr. and Mrs. Veneering and baby.
Mr. Twemlow.   Lord Snigsworthy.   Boots and
Brewer.   Mr. and Mrs. Podsnap.   Analytical
chemist.   Retainer.   Lady Tippins.   Eugene
Wrayburn.   The Two Buffers.   Mortimer Light-
wood.   John Harmon.
Chap. 3.—Charley Hexam.   Inspector.   Julius
Handford.   Job Potterson, ship's steward.   Jacob
Kibble, passenger.
Chap. 4.—Mr. Reginald Wilfer—the Cherub.
Mrs. Wilfer.   Bella and Lavinia Wilfer.   George
Sampson.   John Rokesmith (alias Julius Hand-
ford).
Chap. 5.—Silas Wegg.   Uncle Parker.   Miss
Elizabeth.   Master George.   Aunt Jane.   Mr.
and Mrs. Boffin.   Boffin's Bower.
Chap. 6.—Miss Abbey Potterson, landlady of the
" Six Jolly Fellowship Porters."   Bob Glibbery.
Rogue Riderhood (f.m. 1.)   Tom Tootle.   Capt.
Joey.   Bob Glamour.   William Williams.   Jack
Mullins.   George Jones.   Jonathan.
Chap. 7.—Mr. Venus.
Chap. 8.—Blight, Mortimer Lightwood's clerk.
Chap. 9.—Rev. Frank Milvey and Mrs. Milvey.
Chap. 10.—Sophronia   Akershem   and   Alfred
Lammle (f.m. 2.)   Medusa, Sophronia's aunt.

Chap. 11.—Miss Georgiana Podsnap. The Foreign Gentlemen. Mr. Grompus.

Chap. 16.—Betty Higden. Sloppy. Poddles and Toddles, her nurse children.

BOOK THE SECOND

Chap. 1.—Bradley Headstone, schoolmaster. Miss Peecher, schoolmistress. Mary Anne, pupil. Fanny Cleaver (Jenny Wren), the doll's dressmaker.

Chap. 2.—Dolls, Jenny Wren's father.

Chap. 3.—Pocket-Breaches.

Chap. 4.—Mr. Fascination Fledgeby.

Chap. 5.—Pubsey and Co. Riah, the Jew.

Chap. 12.—Pleasant Riderhood. George Radfoot.

BOOK THE FOURTH

Chap. 4.—Gruff and Glum, the Greenwich pensioner.

Chap. 11.—Mrs. Sprodgkin.

Chap. 17.—Chairman. Contractor. Guests of Veneerings.

EDWIN DROOD, 1870. Unfinished.

Chap. 1.—The Chinaman. Lascar and Old Woman.

Chap. 2—Rev. Septimus Crisparkle, Minor Canon. Mr. Tope, chief verger. Mrs. Tope. The Dean. Mr. Jasper, choirmaster. Edwin Drood, his nephew. "Pussey."

Chap. 3.—Cloisterham.   Miss   Twinkelton's school.   Mrs. Tisher.   Foolish Mr. Porters.   Rosa Bud, pupil at the Nuns House (f.m. 2.)

Chap. 4.—Mr. Thomas Sapsea, auctioneer.   Durdles, stonemason.

Chap. 5.—Deputy.   The Traveller's Twopenny.

Chap. 6.—Mrs. Crisparkle.   Mr. Luke Honeythunder.   Neville and Helena Landless.

Chap. 9.—Mr. Grewgious, Rosa's guardian.

Chap. 11.—Bazzard, Mr. Grewgious's clerk.

Chap. 17.—Mr. Tartar.

Chap. 18.—Mr. Dick Datchery.   The Crozier.

Chap. 22.—Mrs. Billicken, lodging house keeper. Lobley, Tartar's man.

"SUNDAY UNDER THREE HEADS," 1836.

I.—*As It Is.*
II.—*As Sabbath Bills Would Make It.*
III.—*As It Might Be Made.*

SKETCHES OF YOUNG GENTLEMEN, 1838.

The Bashful Young Gentleman.—Mr. Hopkins. His sister Harriet.   Mr. Lambert.

The Out And Out Young Gentleman.—Mr. Dummins.   Mr. Warmint Blake.

The Very Friendly Young Gentleman.—Mr. Mincin.   Mr. and Mrs. Capper.   The Martins.   The Watsons.

The Military Young Gentleman.—Colonel Fitz Sordust.

The Political Young Gentleman.

The Domestic Young Gentleman.—Mr. Nixon. His mother. Julia Thompson. The Misses Grey.

The Censorious Young Gentleman.—Mr. Fairfax. Miss Greenwood. Miss Marshall. Mrs. Barker. Mrs. Thompson.

The Funny Young Gentleman.—Mr. Griggins.

The Theatrical Young Gentleman.—Flimkins, Boozle. Mr. Fitzball. Mr. Liston. Mr. Baker, Mr. George Bennett and other actors.

The Poetical Young Gentleman.—John Milkwash.

The Throwing-off Young Gentleman.—Mr. Caveton. Miss Lowfield.

The Young Ladies' Young Gentleman.—Mr. Balim.

SKETCHES OF YOUNG COUPLES, 1840.

The Young Couple.—Miss Emma Fielding. Mr. Harvey. Mr. John. Jane Adams. Anne, from No. 6.

The Formal Couple.

The Loving Couple.—Mr. and Mrs. Leaver. Mrs. Starling.

The Contradictory Couple.—Mrs. Bluebottle's dinner party. Mr. Jenkins. Morgan. Mrs. Parsons. James and Charlotte.

The Couple Who Dote on Their Children.—Mr. and Mrs. Whiffler and children. Mr. Saunders, visitor.

The Cool Couple.—Charles and Louisa.

The Plausible Couple.—Mr. and Mrs. Bobtail

Widger.   The Clickits.   Mr. and Mrs. Jackson.
Mr. Slummery.   Mr. Frithers.   Mrs. Tablewick.
Mrs. Finching.

The Nice Little Couple.—Mr. and Mrs. Chirrup.

The Egotistical Couple.—Mr. and Mrs. Sliver-
stone.   Mr. and Mrs. Briggs.   Sir Chipkins Glog-
wood.   Lord Slang.   Dowager Lady Snorflerer.

The Couple Who Coddle Themselves.—Mr. and
Mrs. Merrywinkle.   Mrs. Chopper.

The Old Couple.—Mr. and Mrs. Harvey.   Crofts,
the barber.

THE MUDFOG PAPERS, 1837.

Public Life of Mr. Tulrumble (once Mayor of
Mudfog).—Mudfog.   Nicholas Tulrumble.   Mrs.
Tulrumble.   Mr. Sniggs.   Edward Twigger.   Mrs.
Twigger.   Mr. Jennings, secretary to Mr. Tul-
rumble.   Mr. Tulrumble, jun.   " The Jolly Boat-
men."   " Lighterman's Arms."

*Full Report of the First Meeting of the Mudfog
Association for the Advancement of Everything.*—
Professors Snore, Doze, and Wheezy.   Mr. Slug.
The " Pig and Tinder Box."   " Original Pig."
Mr. Woodensconce.   Professors Muff and Nogo.
Mr. Wigsby.   Mr. Blunderum.   Dr. Kutan-
kumagen.   Dr. Toorell.   Dr. Fee.   Dr. Nee-
shawts.   Dr. Knight-Bell.   Mr. Ledbrain.   Mr.
Timbered.   Mr. Carter.   Mr. Truck.   Mr. Wag-
horn.   Professor Queerspeck.   Mr. Jobba.

Full Report of the Second Meeting of the Mudfog

Association for the Advancement of Everything.—
Professor Grime.   The " Black Boy and Stomach-
ache."   The " Boot-jack and Countenance."   Dr.
Foxey.   Mr. Muddlebranes.   Mr. Drawley.   Mr.
X Misty.   Mr. X X Misty.   Mr. Purblind.   Pro-
fessor Rummun.   The Hon. and Rev. Mr. Long
Eers.   Professor John Ketch.   Sir William Jolter-
hed.   Dr. Buffer.   Mr. Smith, of London.   Mr.
Brown, of Edinburgh.   Sir Hookham Snivey.   Pro-
fessor Pumpkinskull.   Sowster, the beadle.   Mr.
Kwakley.   Mr. Flummery.   Mr. Mallett.   Messrs.
Leaver and Scroo.   Mr. Crinkles.   Mr. Copper-
nose.   Mr. Fogle Hunter.   Mr. Tickle.   Mr. Blank.
Mr. Prosee.   Dr. Soemup.   Messrs. Pessell and
Mortair.   Dr. Grummidge.   Mr. Pipkin.   Messrs.
Noakes and Styles.   Mr. Grub.   Messrs. Dull
and Dummy.   Captain Blunderbore.   **Mr. Q. J.**
Snuffletoffle.   Mr. Blubb.

The Pantomime of Life.—March, 1837.—Hon.
Capt. Fitz-Whisker Fiercy.   Do'em, his man.

Some Particulars Concerning a Lion.—May, 1837.

Mr. Robert Bolton.—Mr. Clip.   Mr. Murgatroyd.
Mr. Thickness.   Mr. Sawyer.

PLAYS.

THE VILLAGE COQUETTES, 1836.

Squire Norton.   Hon. Sparkins Flam, friend.
Old Benson, farmer.   Mr. Martin Stokes, farmer.
George Edmunds.   Young Benson.   John Maddox.
Lucy Benson.   Rose, her cousin.

THE STRANGE GENTLEMAN, 1836.

Mrs. Noakes.   Waiters.   The Strange Gentleman.   Tom Sparks.   Mary and Fanny Wilson.
John Johnson.   Charles Tomkins.   Julia Dobbs.
Overton.   Chambermaid.

IS SHE HIS WIFE? OR SOMETHING SINGULAR.

Alfred Lovetown.   Mr. Peter Limbury.   Felix
Tapkins, Esq.   John, servant to Lovetown.   Mrs.
Lovetown.   Mrs. Peter Limbury.

THE LAMPLIGHTER, 1838.

Mr. Stargazer.   Master Galileo Isaac Newton
Hamsted Stargazer, his son.   Tom Grig, the lamp-
lighter.   Mr. Mooney, astrologer.   Servant.   Betsy
Martin.   Emma Stargazer.   Fanny Brown.

CONTRIBUTIONS TO CHRISTMAS
NUMBERS OF HOUSEHOLD WORDS

THE SEVEN POOR TRAVELLERS, 1854.

In the Old City of Rochester.   Richard Watts's
Charity.   The Matron.   The Travellers.

The First.—Richard Doubledick.   Mary Marshall.   Captain Taunton and his mother.   The
French Officer.   Ben, the wall-eyed young man.
The Road.

THE HOLLY TREE INN, 1855.

The Guest.—Myself, Charley. Angela Leath. Edwin.

The Boots.—Master Harry Walmers. Cobbs. Norah. Mr. Walmers.

The Bill.—Emmeline.

THE WRECK OF THE GOLDEN MARY, 1856.

The Wreck.—Captain George William Ravender, commander. John Steadiman, chief mate. Smithick and Watersby, merchants. Tom Snow, steward. Mr. William Rames, second mate. John Mullion. Mr. Rarx. Mrs. Atherfield and child, Lucy, and Miss Coleshaw, passengers.

THE PERILS OF CERTAIN ENGLISH PRISONERS, 1857

The Island of Silver Store.—Gill Davis. Harry Charker, privates. Lieutenant Linderwood, officer. Christian George King, pilot. Sergeant Drooce. Captain Maryon. Captain Carton. Tom Packer. Mr. and Mrs. Commissioner Pordage. Mrs. Belltott. Mr. Kitten. Miss Marion Maryon. Mrs. Venning. Mr. Fisher. Mrs. Fanny Fisher. Mr. and Mrs. Macey. The Pirates. Portuguese Captain.

The Rafts on the River.

A HOUSE TO LET, 1858

Going Into Society.—Toby Magsman, showman. Major Tpschoffki or Chops, the dwarf. Normandy. The Indian. The Fat Lady from Norfolk.

ALL THE YEAR ROUND

THE HAUNTED HOUSE, 1859

The Mortals in the House.—The Goggle-eyed Gentleman in train.

Landlord at Inn. The Poplars. "Ikey" Perkins, general dealer. The hooded woman with the Owl. Master B. The Odd Girl. Cook. Streaker, housemaid. Bottles, stableman. "John," myself and sister Patty. John Herschell, cousin. Alfred Starling and wife. Belinda Bates. Jack Governor. Nat Beaver. Mr. Undery.

The Ghost in Master B.'s Room.—The Spectre. Old Doylance. Miss Griffin. Miss Bule. Miss Pipson. Mesrour. The Seraglio. Grand Vizier.

A MESSAGE FROM THE SEA, 1860

The Village.—Steepways. Captain Jorgan. Tom Pettifer, young fisherman. Mrs. Raybrock. Alfred Raybrock. Hugh Raybrock. His wife, Margaret, "Kitty."

The Money.—Mr. Tregarthen, Kitty's father. David Polreath. Penrewen. John Tredgear and Arson Parvis, old residents of Lanrean.

The Restitution.—Lawrence Clissold, clerk in office of Dringworth Brothers.

TOM TIDDLER'S GROUND, 1861

Picking up Soot and Cinders.—Mr. Mopes, the Hermit. Mr. Traveller. Landlord of "Peal of Bells" Inn. The Tinker.

Picking up Miss Kimmeens.—Miss Pupford. Miss Pupford's assistant and pupils. Miss Linx. "G." Kitty Kimmeens. The Cook. House-maid Bella.
Picking up the Tinker.

SOMEBODY'S LUGGAGE, 1862

His Leaving It Till Called For.—Christopher, myself, head waiter. Joseph, head waiter at Slamjam Coffee House. "Old Charles." Mrs. Pratchett, head chambermaid. The Mistress. Miss Martin at the Bar.
His Boots.—Monsieur Mutuel. Madame Bou-clet. Mr. Langley. Vauban. The Physician's Daughter. Private Valentine. Private Hyppo-lite. Monsieur le Capitaine de la Cour. Emile. Eugene. Baptiste. Corporal Theophile. The Barber. Little Bebelle.
His Brown Paper Parcel.—"Tom" (in Fine Art Line). Mr. Click. The Street Artist. Henrietta.
His Wonderful End.

MRS. LIRRIPER'S LODGINGS, 1863

How Mrs. Lirriper Carried On The Business.— Mrs. Emma Lirriper. Miss Wozenham. Mr. Betley, lodger. Wandering Christians. Willing Sophy. Mary Ann Perkinsop and Caroline Maxey, servants. Major Jackman, lodger. Mr. and Mrs. Edson, lodgers. "Jemmy," the boy.
How The Parlours Added a Few Words.

MRS. LIRRIPER'S LEGACY, 1864

How She Went On And Went Over.—Joshua
Lirriper, brother-in-law.   Mr. Buffle, assessed tax
collector.   Mrs. Buffle.   Miss Buffle and Articled
Young Gentleman.   Sally Rairyganoo and Wini-
fred Madgers, servants.   The French gentleman
from the Consul.   The prowling young man at Paris.
Sens.   The Military Character.   The Englishman.
How Jemmy Topped Up.

DR. MARIGOLD'S PRESCRIPTIONS, 1865.

To Be Taken Immediately.—Dr. William Mari-
gold, Cheap Jack.   His wife.   His child, Sophy.
His dog.   Pickleson, the giant.   Mim, his master.
Sophy, Mim's step-daughter, deaf and dumb.
To Be Taken With a Grain of Salt.—The Writer.
The two figures in Piccadilly.   John Derrick,
writer's servant.   The Jury.   Mr. Harker, officer.
The Murderer.   The Appearance.   The Judge.
To Be Taken For Life.—Sophy's husband, the
deaf and dumb young man, and child.

MUGBY JUNCTION, 1866

Barbox Brothers.—The Guard.   Barbox Brothers.
Mugby Junction.   Lamps.   Young Mr. Jackson.
The Children from school.   Phoebe, Lamps' daugh-
ter.
Barbox Brothers and Co.—Polly.   Beatrice,
Polly's mother.   "Melluka," the doll.   Tresham,
Polly's father.

Main Line. The Boy At Mugby.—The Refreshment Room. Papers. Our Missis. Bandolining Room. Miss Whiff. Miss Piff. Mrs. Sniff. Mr. Sniff. Ezekiel, assistants.

No. 1 Branch Line. The Signalman.—The Signalman and the Spectre.

NO THOROUGHFARE, 1867

The Overture.—The Foundling Hospital. Sally, a nurse. The Veiled Lady. Walter Wilding, foundling.

Act I. The Curtain Rises.—Wilding and Co., wine merchants. Mr. Bintrey, lawyer. Joey Ladle, head cellarman. Pebbleson, Nephew.

Enter The Housekeeper.—Jarvis. Mrs. Goldstraw.

The Housekeeper Speaks.—George Vendale.

New Characters On The Scene.—Defresnier et Cie. M. Jules Obenreizer. His niece, Marguerite. Madame Dor.

Act II. Vendale Makes Love.—The Speechless Friend.

Act IV. The Clock Lock.—Maitre Voigt, the notary, of Neuchatel.

MISCELLANEOUS PAPERS

THE LAZY TOUR OF TWO IDLE APPRENTICES

Published in " Household Words " for October, 1857

Chap. 1.—Mr. Thomas Idle. Mr. Francis Goodchild. Mr. Podgers. Mr. Codgers. The Innkeeper.

5

Chap. 2.—The Landlady. Jock. Dr. Speddie. Mr. Lorn, his assistant. Arthur Holliday. The " Two Robins " Inn. Ben. The Landlord. The Medical Student.

Chap. 3.—Allonby. Lancaster.

Chap. 4.—The Bride. The Old Man. Dick.

HUNTED DOWN

Published in " All the Year Round," 1860.

Part II.—Mr. Julius Slinkton, of Middle Temple. Mr. Sampson, Chief Manager of a Life Insurance Company. Mr. Adams, clerk to same. Mr. Meltham, Actuary of the " Inestimable."

Part III.—Mr. Alfred Beckwith, the insured.

Part IV.—Miss Margaret Niner (niece to Mr. Slinkton). Major Banks, East India Director.

A HOLIDAY ROMANCE

Published in " All the Year Round," 1868

Part. 1.—Rob Redforth. Nettie Ashford. Alice Rainbird. The Misses Drowvey and Grimmer. William Tinkling.

Part 2.—King and Queen Watkins. The Princess Alicia, their eldest daughter. Mr. Pickles, fishmonger, and boy. The Good Fairy. Grandmarina. Peggy, the Lord Chamberlain. The Duchess. Peacocks. Prince Certainpersonio.

Part 3.—Captain Boldheart. The Beauty, schooner. Bill Boozey. Scorpion, boat. The Family of Boldheart. The Mayor of Margate.

Part 4.—Mrs. Orange. Tootelum Boots. Mrs.

Lemon. Emilia. White. Brown. Mrs. Black. Mr. Orange. Mrs. Alicumpanie.

GEORGE SILVERMAN'S EXPLANATION

Published in " All the Year Round " for 1868.

Chap. 4.—Mr. Verity. Brother Hawkyard, of West Bromwich. Hoghton Towers.
Chap. 5.—Silvia.
Chap. 6.—Brother Gimblet. Brother Parksop.
Chap. 7.—Mr. Fareway. Lady Fareway. Sir Gaston Fareway. Adelina.
Chap. 9.—Mr. Granville Wharton.

REPRINTED PIECES.

The Long Voyage.

Captain Bligh. Fletcher Christian. **The** Halsewell, East Indiaman and passengers. Captain Pierce and daughters. Messrs. Rogers, Brimer and Meriton, mates. Mr. Schutz, passenger. Mr. Macmanus, midshipman. Miss Mansel. **The** Grosvenor.

The Begging Letter Writer.

A Child's Dream of a Star.

Our English Watering Place.

The Assembly Rooms. Miss Julia Mills. Hon. Miss Peepy.

Our French Watering Place.

Monsieur Loyal Devasseur.   Mons. Feroce.

Bill Sticking.

The King of the Bill Stickers.

Births.—Mrs. Meek, Of A Son.

Mr. and Mrs. Meek, Maria Jane.   Mrs. Bigby,
mother-in-law.   Mrs. Prodgit, nurse.   Augustus
George Meek, infant.

Lying Awake.

The Poor Relation's Story.

John, host.   Little Frank.   Uncle Chill.   Christiana.   John Spatter, clerk.   Betsy Snap.   Michael,
poor relation.

The Child's Story.

The Schoolboy's Story.

Old Cheeseman.   The Reverend.   Jane Pitt.   Bob
Tartar.

Nobody's Story.

The Bigwig family.

The Ghost of Art.

The Model.   Mrs. Parkins.

Out of Town.

Pavilionstone.   Great Pavilionstone Hotel.

Out of the Season.

Admiral Benbow.   Mr. Clocker.   Mrs. B. Wedgington, and family.

A Poor Man's Tale of a Patent.

Old John.   William Butcher.   Thomas Joy.

The Noble Savage.

A Flight.

Trip to Paris.   Fellow passengers.

The Detective Police.

Inspectors Wield and Stalker.   Sergeants Dornton, Witcham, Mith, Fendall and Straw.   Tally-Ho Thompson.   Mr. Thomas Pidgeon.   Fikey. The Butcher's Story.   The Adventures of a carpet bag.   Mescheck.   Dr. Dunday.

Three Detective Anecdotes.

1st.—The Pair of Gloves.   Eliza Grimwood. Mr. Trinkle.   Messrs. Phibbs, Wield, Dornton, Mith.

2nd.—The Artful Touch.   Sergeant Witchem, Inspector Wield, Mr. Tatt.   The Swell Mob.

3rd.—The Sofa.

On Duty With Inspector Field.

Rats Castle.   Lodging Houses and inmates.

Down With The Tide.

Peacoat.   Waterloo.

A Walk in the Workhouse.

Inmates.

Prince Bull. A Fairy Tale.

Fair Freedom.   Tape.   Prince Bear.

A Plated Article.

Our Honorable Friend.

The Member for Verbosity.   Tipkisson, the saddler.

Our School.

Miss Frost.   Master Mawls.   Dumbledon. Maxby and his sisters.   Mr. Blinkins, the Latin master.   The Chief and ushers.   Phil.

Our Vestry.

Mr. Magg.   Mr. Wigsby.   Mr. Tiddypot.   Captain Banger.   Mr. Chib.

Our Bore.

Blumb.   Pierre Blanquo.   Jilkins.   Callow. Moon, Parkins, etc.

A Monument of French Folly.

The Cattle Markets and Abattoirs.

The Christmas Tree.

CHRISTMAS BOOKS.

A CHRISTMAS CAROL, 1843

Stave 1st.—Ebenezer Scrooge. Jacob Marley. Scrooge's nephew, Fred. Scrooge's clerk, Bob Cratchit. Two philanthropic gentlemen. Jacob Marley's Ghost.

Stave 2nd.—Little Fan, Scrooge's sister. Old Fezziwig, Scrooge's former master. Mrs. Fezziwig. Three Misses Fezziwig. Dick Wilkins.

Stave 3rd.—Mrs. Cratchit. Belinda. Martha. Peter Cratchit and Tiny Tim. Scrooge's niece and her sisters. Topper.

Stave 4th.—Old Joe, rag dealer. Mrs. Dilber, laundress.

THE CHIMES, 1844

First quarter.—Toby or Trotty Veck, porter. Meg, his daughter. Richard, Meg's sweetheart. Alderman Cute. Mr. Filer.

Second quarter.—Sir Joseph Bowley. Lady Bowley. Mr. Fish, secretary. Deedles, banker. Will Fern. Mrs. Chickenstalker, Toby's landlady. Lillian, Will Fern's niece.

Third quarter.—The Bells.

Fourth quarter.—Mr. Tugby.

THE CRICKET ON THE HEARTH, 1845

Chirp 1st.—John Peerybingle, carrier. Mrs. Dot Peerybingle and baby. Tilly Slowboy, maid.

Boxer, dog.   Gruff and Tackleton, toy merchants.
Caleb Plummer.   The Old Gentleman.
   Chirp 2nd.—Bertha Plummer, the blind girl.
May Fielding and her mother.
   Chirp 3rd.—Edward Plummer (f.m. 1.)

THE BATTLE OF LIFE, 1846

   Part 1st.—Dr. Jeddler.   His daughters, Grace
and Marion.   Alfred Heathfield, Marion's lover.
Benjamin Britain and Clemency Newcome, ser-
vants.   Messrs. Snitchey and Craggs, lawyers.
   Part 2nd.—Mrs. Craggs.   Mrs. Snitchey.
Michael Warden.

THE HAUNTED MAN, 1848

   Chap. 1.—Mr. Redlaw, chemist.   Mr. William
Swidger.   Mrs. William Swidger, Milly.   Philip
Swidger, father.   The boy.   The Phantom.
   Chap. 2.—Mr. Tetterby, newsman.   Mrs. Tet-
terby and family.   Mr. Denham, student, alias
Edmund Longford.   His bride.   George Swidger.

PART THREE

Complete Alphabetical Index

PART THREE

Complete Alphabetical Index.

A

Character or place.	Book	Chap.
Abbaye, prison of ...	Tale Of Two Cities Book 2	24
Absent, City of the ...	Uncommercial Traveller	21
Adams	David Copperfield	16
Adams, Jane	Sketches, Young Couples The Young Couple	
Adams, Mr.	Hunted Down	2
Adelina	Geo. Silverman's Explanation	7
Admiralty	Little Dorrit, Book 1	21
Advocate	Uncommercial Traveller	28
Affery	Little Dorrit, Book 1	3
African Knife Swallower	Nicholas Nickleby	48

Character or place.	Book.	Chap.
Aged Parent	Great Expectations	25
Agnes	David Copperfield	15
Agnes—"Boz." ...	The Boarding House	2
Akerman Mr.	Barnaby Rudge	64
Akershem, Sophronia	Our Mutual Friend Book 1	10
Allen, Arabella	Pickwick	28
Allen, Benjamin ...	Pickwick	30
Alicumpaine	Holiday Romance	4
Alice, Mistress	Master Humphrey's Clock	1
Almshouses, Titbull's	Uncommercial Traveller	27
Alphonse	Nicholas Nickleby	21
Amateur Beat, On an	Uncommercial Traveller	34
Amazon, The	Uncommercial Traveller	20
Amelia and Jane— "Boz."	Tuggs's At Ramsgate	
American Characteristics	American Notes	18
American Railroads ...	American Notes	4
Analytical Chemist ...	Our Mutual Friend Book 1	2
Angel, The	Pickwick	16
Anglo-Bengalee Company	Martin Chuzzlewit	27
Anne	Sketches Young Couples —The Young Couple	
Anny	Oliver Twist	24
Antonio	Pictures From Italy	

Character or place.	*Book.*	*Chap.*
Apothecary, The ...	Dombey And Son	14
Apothecary, Apprentice	Oliver Twist	24
Apparitor—"Boz." ...	Doctors Commons	
Apprentices—"Boz."	Characters	1
Artful Dodger, The ...	Oliver Twist	8
Article, A Plated ...	Reprinted Pieces	
Ashford, Nettie	Holiday Romance	1
Asylums	American Notes	3 and 5
Atherfield, Mrs	Wreck of the Golden Mary	1
Astley's—"Boz." ...	Scenes	11
Attorney General ...	Tale Of Two Cities Book 2	2
Aunt, Mr F's	Little Dorrit, Book 1	13
Aunt, The Allens' ...	Pickwick	48
Avenger, The	Great Expectations	27
Avignon, Goblin of ...	Pictures From Italy	
Avvocato	Pictures From Italy	
Ayresleigh, Mr.	Pickwick	40

B

Badger (Bayham) Mr. and Mrs	Bleak House	13
Badger, The Black ...	Dombey And Son	22
Bagman's story	Pickwick	14
Bagman, One-eyed ...	Pickwick	48
Bagnet family	Bleak House	27
Bagstock, Major ...	Dombey And Son	7
Bailey junr.	Chuzzlewit	9

Character or place.	Book.	Chap.
Bailey, Capt	David Copperfield	18
Baker, Mr	Uncommercial Traveller	3
Baker, Mr	Sketches, Young Gents—The Theatrical	
Balderstone, Mr T.—"Boz."	Mrs. J. Porter	
Balim, Mr	Sketches, Young Gents—The Young Ladies'	
Baltimore	American Notes	8
Bamber, Jack	Pickwick	20
Bambino	Pictures From Italy	
Banger, Capt	Reprinted Pieces—Our Vestry	
Bangham, Mrs	Little Dorrit, Book 1	6
Bank Clerk	Nicholas Nickleby	37
Banks	Uncommercial Traveller	21
Banks, Major	Hunted Down	4
Bantam, Angelo Cyrus	Pickwick	35
Baps, Mr. and Mrs.	Dombey And Son	14
Baptiste	Somebody's Luggage—His Boots	
"Bar"	Little Dorrit, Book 1	21
Barbara	Old Curiosity Shop	22
Barbara's mother ...	Old Curiosity Shop	39
Barbary, Miss	Bleak House	3
Barber, The	Somebody's Luggage—His Boots	
Barber, The	Master Humphrey's Clock	1

Character or place.	*Book.*	*Chap.*
Barbox Brothers ...	Mugby Junction	
Bardell, Mrs. and Master	Pickwick	12
Bargemen, Three Jolly	Great Expectations	10
Barker, Phil	Oliver Twist	26
Barker, W.—"Boz."	Scenes	17
Barker, Mr.	Sketches, Young Gents - The Censorious	
Barkis, Mr.	David Copperfield	5
Barley, Old, and Clara Barley	Great Expectations	46
Barlow, Mr.	Uncommercial Traveller	33
Barnacle family	Little Dorrit, Book 1	10
Barnacle, Lord Decimus	Little Dorrit, Book 1	13
Barnacle Tite	Little Dorrit, Book 1	9
Barnacles, various ...	Little Dorrit, Book 1	26 and 34
Barney	Oliver Twist	15
Baron of Grogswig ...	Nicholas Nickleby	6
Barroneau, Monsr. and Madame	Little Dorrit, Book 1	1
Barton, Mr.—"Boz"	Horatio Sparkins	
Barsad, John	Tale Of Two Cities, Book 2	3
Bachelor, The	Old Curiosity Shop	52
Bates, Charley	Oliver Twist	9
Bates, Belinda	Haunted House, Mortals	
Battens, Mr.	Uncommercial Traveller	27
Bazzard	Edwin Drood	11

Character or place.	Book.	Chap.
Beadle, The	Bleak House	11
Bear, Prince	Reprinted Pieces—Prince Bull	
Beatrice	Mugby Junction (Barbox Bros. and Co.)	
Beaver, Nat	Haunted House, Mortals In The House	
Bebelle, Little	Somebody's Luggage—His Boots	
Beckwith, Alfred ...	Hunted Down	3
Bedwin, Mrs.	Oliver Twist	12
Begging Letter Writer	Reprinted Pieces	
Belinda	Master Humphrey's Clock	2
Bella	Tom Tiddler's Ground	6
Bellamy's—" Boz " ...	Scenes	18
Belleville	American Notes	13
Belling	Nicholas Nickleby	4
Bellows, Brother ...	Little Dorrit, Book 1	21
Bells, The	Chimes, 3rd quarter	
Belvawney, Miss ...	Nicholas Nickleby	23
Benbow, Admiral ...	Reprinted Pieces—Out Of The Season	
Ben	Lazy Tour Of Two Idle Apprentices	2
Ben	Seven Poor Travellers	1
Bennett, Mr. George ...	Sketches, Young Gents—Theatrical	
Benson, Old and Young and Lucy	Village Coquettes	

Character or place.	Book.	Chap.
Benton, Miss	Master Humphrey's Clock	6
Berinthia	Dombey And Son	8
Bethel, Little	Old Curiosity Shop	41
Betley, Mr.	Mrs. Lirriper's Lodgings	1
Betsy	Oliver Twist	9
Bevan, Mr.	Martin Chuzzlewit	17
Bevis Marks	Old Curiosity Shop	11
Bib, J. W. M.	Martin Chuzzlewit	34
Biddy	Great Expectations	7
Bigby	Reprinted Pieces—Births	
Bigwig	Reprinted Pieces—Nobody's Story	
Bilberry, Lady	Little Dorrit, Book 1	17
Biler	Dombey And Son	2
Billickin, Mrs.	Edwin Drood	22
Billsmethi Signor—"Boz"	Dancing Academy	
Bilson and Slum	Pickwick	14
Bintrey, Mr.	No Thoroughfare, Act 1—The Curtain Rises	
Birmingham, Mr. and Mrs.	Uncommercial Traveller	17
Birthday celebrations	Uncommercial Traveller	19
Bishop	Little Dorrit, Book 1	21
Bitherston, Master	Dombey And Son	8
Bitzer	Hard Times, Book 1	2
Black, Mrs.	Holiday Romance	4

6

Character or place.	Book.	Chap.
Blackboy and Stomachache	Mudfog Papers, 2nd Meeting	
Blackmore—" Boz "	Vauxhall Gardens	
Blackpool, Stephen and wife	Hard Times, Book 1	10
Bladud, Legend of Prince	Pickwick	36
Blake, Mr. Warmint...	Sketches, Young Gents— The Out And Out	
Blandois, Monsr. ...	Little Dorrit, Book 1	30
Blank, Mr.	Mudfog Papers, 2nd Meeting	
Blanquo, Pierre ...	Reprinted Pieces— Our Bore	
Blathers	Oliver Twist	31
Bleeding Heart Yard	Little Dorrit, Book 1	9
Bligh, Capt.	Reprinted Pieces— Long Voyage	
Blight, Young	Our Mutual Friend, Book 1	8
Blimber, Dr., Mrs. and Cornelia ...	Dombey And Son	11
Blinder, Mrs.	Bleak House	15
Blinkins, Mr.	Reprinted Pieces— Our School	
Blockitt, Mrs.	Dombey And Son	1
Blockson, Mrs. ...	Nicholas Nickleby	18
Bloss, Mrs.—" Boz."	The Boarding House	2
Blotton, Mr.	Pickwick	1
Blue Dragon, Salisbury	Martin Chuzzlewit	2

Character or place.	*Book.*	*Chap.*
Bluebottle, Mrs. ...	Sketches, Young Couples—Contradictory	
Blubb, Mr.	Mudfog Papers, 2nd Meeting	
Blumb	Reprinted Pieces— Our Bore	
Blunderbore, Capt. ...	Mudfog Papers, 2nd Meeting	
Blunderem, Mr. ...	Mudfog Papers 1st Meeting	
Blunderstone	David Copperfield	1
Boar (Blue)	Pickwick	33
Boatmen	Old Curiosity Shop	43
Bob, the Turnkey ...	Little Dorrit, Book 1	6
Bobster, Cecilia ...	Nicholas Nickleby	40
Boffin, Mr. and Mrs. and Boffin's Bower ...	Our Mutual Friend, Book 1	5
Bogsby	Bleak House	33
Bogus, Mr. and Mrs.	Uncommercial Traveller	6
Boiled Beef of New England	Uncommercial Traveller	23
Boiler (Boanerges) ...	Uncommercial Traveller	9
Bokum, Mrs.	Dombey And Son	60
Bolder	Nicholas Nickleby	8
Boldheart, Capt. ...	Holiday Romance	3
Boldwig, Capt. ...	Pickwick	19
Boles and Coles ...	Uncommercial Traveller	12

Character or place.	Book.	Chap.
Bolo, Miss	Pickwick	35
Bologna Cemetery ...	Pictures From Italy	
Bolter, Morris	Oliver Twist	42
Bolton, Mr.	Robert Bolton	
Bonney	Nicholas Nickleby	2
Boodle, Lord	Bleak House	12
Borrioboola-Gha ...	Bleak House	4
Boot-Jack, The, and Countenance ...	Mudfog Papers, 2nd Meeting	
Boots—" Boz." ...	Winglebury Duel	
Boots and Brewer ...	Our Mutual Friend, Book 1	2
Boozey, Bill	Holiday Romance	3
Boozle	Sketches, Young Gents— The Theatrical	
Borum, Mrs.	Nicholas Nickleby	24
Boston	American Notes	3
Bottle of Wine ...	Uncommercial Travel- ler	28
Bottles	Haunted House—Mor- tals In The House	
Bouclet, Madame ...	Somebody's Luggage— His Boots	
Bounderby, Mr. ...	Hard Times, Book 1	4
Bowley, Sir Joseph and Lady	Chimes, 2nd quarter	
Bowyer, The	Master Humphrey's Clock	1
Boxer	Cricket On The Hearth	1
Boy, The	Haunted Man	1
Boylston School ...	American Notes	3

Character or place.	Book.	Chap.
Brandley, Mrs. and Miss	Great Expectations	38
Brass Sally	Old Curiosity Shop	33
Brass, Sampson ...	Old Curiosity Shop	11
Bravassa, Miss	Nicholas Nickleby	23
Bray, Mr. and Madeline	Nicholas Nickleby	46
Break of Day	Little Dorrit, Book 1	11
Brick, Jefferson, Mr. and Mrs.	Martin Chuzzlewit	16
Brick Lane Branch, etc.	Pickwick	33
Brickmakers, The ...	Bleak House	8
Bridgeman, Laura ...	American Notes	3
Brig Place	Dombey And Son	9
Briggs	Dombey And Son	12
Briggs, Mr. and Mrs.	Sketches, Young Couples—The Egotistical	
Briggs' family— " Boz."	Steam Excursion	
Brimer Mr.	Reprinted Pieces— Long Voyage	
Britain, Benjamin ...	Battle Of Life	1
Britannia Theatre ...	Uncommercial Traveller	4
Britannia, The	American Notes	1
Brittles	Oliver Twist	28
Brogley	Dombey And Son	9
Brogson—" Boz." ...	Mr. Minns And His Cousin	
Brooker	Nicholas Nickleby	44

Character or place.	Book.	Chap.
Brook Dingwalls, The —" Boz."	Sentiment	
Brooks of Sheffield ...	David Copperfield	2
Browdie, John	Nicholas Nickleby	9
Brown, Misses— " Boz."	Our Parish	6
Brown, Emily—" Boz "	Winglebury Duel	
Brown, Mr.	Mudfog Papers, 2nd Meeting	
Brown, Fanny	The Lamplighter	
Brown, Mr.—" Boz "	Mrs. J. Porter	
Brown, Mr. Henry— " Boz."	Our Parish	6
Brown	Holiday Romance	4
Brown, Good Mrs. ...	Dombey And Son	6
Brownlow, Mr. ...	Oliver Twist	10
Bucket, Inspector ...	Bleak House	22
Bucket, Mrs.	Bleak House	53
Bud, Rosa	Edwin Drood	3
Budden, Octavius and family—" Boz." ...	Mr. Minns And His Cousin	
Budger, Mrs.	Pickwick	2
Buffer, Dr.	Mudfog Papers, 2nd Meeting	
Buffers, The Two ...	Our Mutual Friend, Book 1	2
Buffey, Hon. W. ...	Bleak House	12
Buffle and family ...	Mrs. Lirriper's Legacy	1
Buffs and Blues ...	Pickwick	13
Buffum, Oscar	Martin Chuzzlewit	34
Bulders	Pickwick	2

Character or place.	Book.	Chap.
Bull Inn, Holborn ...	Martin Chuzzlewit	25
Bull Inn, Rochester ...	Pickwick	2
Bull's Eye	Oliver Twist	16
Bule, Miss	Haunted House— 'Ghost In Master B.'s Room	
Bullamy	Martin Chuzzlewit	27
Bullfinch	Uncommercial Travel- ler	32
Bulph	Nicholas Nickleby	23
Bumble, Mr.	Oliver Twist	2
Bumple and Sludberry —" Boz "	Doctors Commons	
Bung, Mr.—" Boz."	Our Parish	4
Bunsby, Capt.	Dombey And Son	15
Bush Inn, Bristol ...	Pickwick	38
Butcher, W.	Reprinted Pieces— Poor Man's Tale Of A Patent	
Butler, Theodosius— " Boz."	Sentiment	
Butler, Chief, The ...	Little Dorrit, Book 1	21
Buzfuz, Sergeant ...	Pickwick	34

C

Calais Night Mail ...	Uncommercial Travel- ler	17
Calow	Reprinted Pieces— Our Bore	

Character or place.	Book.	Chap.
Calton, Mr.—" Boz "	The Boarding House	1
Camilla	Great Expectations	11
Canal Boats	American Notes	9 and 10
Cape, Mr.—" Boz."	Mrs. J. Porter	
Capper, Mr. and Mrs.	Sketches, Young Gents—The Very Friendly	
Cappucchino, The ...	Pictures From Italy	
Carboy	Bleak House	3
Carker, Mr. James ...	Dombey And Son	4
Carker, John junr. ...	Dombey And Son	6
Carker, Harriet ...	Dombey And Son	22
Carlavero	Uncommercial Traveller	28
Carmagnole	Tale Of Two Cities, Book 3	5
Carnival	Pictures from Italy	
Carpet Bag	Reprinted Pieces—Detective Police	
Carrara	Pictures from Italy	
Carstone, Richard ...	Bleak House	3
Carter, Mr.	Mudfog Papers 1st Meeting	
Carton, Sidney	Tale Of Two Cities, Book 2	3
Carton, Capt.	Perils Of Certain English Prisoners	1
Casby, Christopher Mr.	Little Dorrit, Book 1	12
Cassino	Pictures From Italy	
Caswell, Oliver ...	American Notes	3
Catacombs	Pictures From Italy	
Cathedrals of Florence	Pictures From Italy	

Character or place.	*Book.*	*Chap.*
Cattle Markets	Reprinted Pieces—Monument of French Folly	
Cautious Clara	Dombey And Son	23
Cavalletto, J. B.	Little Dorrit, Book 1	1
Caveton	Sketches, Young Gents - The Throwing Off	
Certainpersonio ...	Holiday Romance	2
Chadband, Mr. and Mrs.	Bleak House	19
Chairman	Our Mutual Friend, Book 4	17
Chambers	Uncommercial Traveller	14
Chancellor, Lord ...	Bleak House	1
Chancery Prisoner	Pickwick	42
Chapel, The—" Boz."	Newgate	
Chaplain	Pickwick	42
Charker	Perils Of Certain English Prisoners	1
Charles, Old	Somebody's Luggage—Leaving It Till Called For	
Charles and Louisa ...	Sketches, Young Couples—The Cool Couple	
Charlotte	Oliver Twist	4
Charlotte	Little Dorrit, Book 2	21
Charter, Royal	Uncommercial Traveller	2

Character or place.	*Book.*	*Chap.*
Chatham Dockyard ...	Uncommercial Travel- ler	24
Cheeryble Brothers ...	Nicholas Nickleby	35
Cheeryble, Frank ...	Nicholas Nickleby	43
Cheeseman, Old ...	Reprinted Pieces— Schoolboy's Story	
Cheggs, Mr. and Miss	Old Curiosity Shop	8
Chelsea Pensioner ...	Uncommercial Travel- ler	27
Chertsey	Oliver Twist	19
Chesney Wold	Bleak House	7
Chester, Edward ...	Barnaby Rudge	1
Chester, Mr.	Barnaby Rudge	10
Chestle, Mr.	David Copperfield	18
Chib, Mr.	Reprinted Pieces— Our Vestry	
Chick, Mr. and Mrs. ...	Dombey And Son 1 and 2	
Chickenstalker, Mrs.	Chimes, 2nd quarter	
Chief	Reprinted Pieces— Our School	
Child's Dream of a Star	Reprinted Pieces	
Child's Story, The ...	Reprinted Pieces	
Childers	Hard Times, Book 1	6
Chill, Uncle	Reprinted Pieces— Poor Relation's Story	
Chillip, Mr.	David Copperfield	1
Chinaman, The	Edwin Drood	1
Chips	Uncommercial Travel- ler	15

Character or place.	*Book.*	*Chap.*
Chirrup, Mr. and Mrs.	Sketches, Young Couples—The Nice Couple	
Chitling, Tom	Oliver Twist	18
Chivery, Mr., Mrs. and Young John	Little Dorrit, Book 1	18
Choke, General	Martin Chuzzlewit	21
Chollop, Hannibal ...	Martin Chuzzlewit	33
Chops	House To Let—Going Into Society	
Chopper, Mrs.	Sketches, Young Couples—Couple Who Coddle Themselves	
Chowser, Colonel ...	Nicholas Nickleby	19
Christiana	Reprinted Pieces—Poor Relation's Story	
Christmas Dinner, A ... "Boz"	Characters	2
Christmas Tree, The ...	Reprinted Pieces	
Christopher	Somebody's Luggage—Leaving It Till Called For	
Chuckster	Old Curiosity Shop	14
Chuffey, Old	Martin Chuzzlewit	11
Churches, City of London	Uncommercial Traveller	9
Chuzzlewit, Diggory, and Toby	Martin Chuzzlewit	1
Chuzzlewit, Old Martin	Martin Chuzzlewit	3
Chuzzlewit, Jonas ...	Martin Chuzzlewit	4

Character or place.	*Book.*	*Chap.*
Chuzzlewit, Martin	Martin Chuzzlewit	5
Chuzzlewit, Anthony ...	Martin Chuzzlewit	4
Chuzzlewit, George, Ned,		
Mrs., daughters	Martin Chuzzlewit	4
Cicero	Martin Chuzzlewit	17
Cicerone	Pictures From Italy	
Cicerone, The Little ...	Pictures From Italy	
Cincinatti	American Notes	11
Circumlocution Office	Little Dorrit, Book 1	10
Clare, Ada	Bleak House	3
Clark, Betsy—" Boz."	Streets By Morning	
Clark, Mr.	Dombey And Son	7
Clarriker	Great Expectations	37
Claypole Noah	Oliver Twist	5
Cleaver, Fanny ...	Our Mutual Friend,	
	Book 1	2
Clennam, Arthur ...	Little Dorrit, Book 1	2
Clennam, Mrs.	Little Dorrit, Book 1	3
Cleopatra	Dombey And Son	21
Clergyman	Pickwick	6
Clergyman	Old Curiosity Shop	52
Clergyman, New—	Our Parish	2
" Boz."		
Clerk, The—" Boz."...	Our Parish	1
Cleverleys, The	Uncommercial Travel-	
	ler	20
Click, Mr.	Somebody's Luggage—	
	His Brown Paper	
	Parcel	
Clickits, The	...Sketches, Young	
	Couples—The Plausible	

Character or place.	Book.	Chap.
Clickett, The "Orfling"	David Copperfield	11
Clifford's Inn	Pickwick	21
Clip, Mr.	Mr Robert Bolton	
Clissold Lawrence ..	Message From The Sea—Restitution	
Clocker, Mr.	Reprinted Pieces—Out of the Season	
Cloisterham	Edwin Drood	3
Club, Pickwick	Pickwick	1
Clubbers, The	Pickwick	2
Cluppins, Mrs.	Pickwick	26
Cly, Roger	Tale Of Two Cities, Book 2	3
Coachmaker	Uncommercial Traveller	22
Coaching House ...	Uncommercial Traveller	22
Coavinses	Bleak House	6
Cobb, Tom	Barnaby Rudge	1
Cobbey	Nicholas Nickleby	8
Cobbler, The	Pickwick	44
Cobbs	Holly Tree Inn—The Boots	
Cocker, Indignation Mr.	Uncommercial Traveller	32
Codger, Miss	Martin Chuzzlewit	34
Codgers, Mr.	Lazy Tour Of Two Idle Apprentices	1
Codlin, Thomas ..	Old Curiosity Shop	16
Coiler, Mrs.	Great Expectations	23
Coketown	Hard Times, Book 1	3

Character or place.	Book.	Chap.
Coleshaw, Miss	Wreck of The Golden Mary	1
Compeyson	Great Expectations	42
Conciergerie	Tale Of Two Cities, Book 3	6
Condemned Cells— "Boz"	Newgate	
Conkey Chickweed ...	Oliver Twist	31
Constables	Oliver Twist	30
Contractor	Our Mutual Friend, Book 4	17
Convent, Great St. Bernard	Little Dorrit, Book 2	1
Convicts	Great Expectations	1
Conway, General ...	Barnaby Rudge	49
Cook, Mrs. Maylie's ...	Oliver Twist	28
Cooking Depots	Uncommercial Traveller	23
Cook's Court, Cursitor Street	Bleak House	10
Cooper, Augustus— "Boz"	Dancing Academy	
Copperfield, Mr. and Mrs.	David Copperfield	1
Copperfield, David ...	David Copperfield	1
Coppernoze, Mr. ...	Mudfog Papers, 2nd Meeting	
Corney Mrs.	Oliver Twist	23
Coroner	Bleak House	11
Coroner's Jury	Uncommercial Traveller	18

Character or place.	Book.	Chap.
Cottagers, The	Old Curiosity Shop	15
Counsel—" Boz " ...	Doctors Commons	
County Justice, The ...	Barnaby Rudge	47
Courier, French The	Pictures From Italy	
Cower, Mrs.—" Boz "	Tuggs's at Ramsgate	
Crackit, Toby	Oliver Twist	19
Craddock, Mrs.	Pickwick	36
Craggs, Mr. and Mrs....	Battle of Life	1 and 2
Cratchit, Bob and family	Christmas Carol	Stave 3
Creakle, Mr., Mrs. and Miss	David Copperfield	5
Crewler, Sophy and Sarah	David Copperfield	34
Crewler, Rev. Horace and Mrs.	David Copperfield	41
Crewler, Misses	David Copperfield	59
Crocus, Dr.	American Notes	13
Crofts	Sketches Young Couples —The Old Couple	
Crookey	Pickwick	40
Crowl, Mr.	Nicholas Nickleby	14
Crozier, The	Edwin Drood	18
Criminal Courts— " Boz "	Scenes	24
Crimple, David	Martin Chuzzlewit	27
Crinkles	Mudfog Papers, 2nd Meeting	
Cripples's Academy ...	Little Dorrit, Book 1	9
Crisparkle, Septimus ...	Edwin Drood	2
Crisparkle, Mrs. ...	Edwin Drood	6

Character or place.	Book.	Chap.
Crummles, Mr. and family	Nicholas Nickleby 22 and 23	
Crumpton, Misses— "Boz"	Sentiment	
Cruncher, Jerry, Mrs. etc.	Tale Of Two Cities, Book 2	1
Crupp, Mrs.	David Copperfield	23
Crushton, Mr.	Pickwick	35
Curate, The—"Boz"	Our Parish	2
Curdle, Mr. and Mrs.	Nicholas Nickleby	24
Curson, Thomas ...	Barnaby Rudge	8
Cutler, Mr. and Mrs.	Nicholas Nickleby	14
Cuttle, Captain	Dombey And Son	4
Cute, Alderman ...	Chimes, 1st quarter	

D

Dadsons, The—"Boz"	Sentiment	
Daisy, Solomon	Barnaby Rudge	1
"Daisy"	David Copperfield	20
Damiens	Tale Of Two Cities, Book, 2	15
Danton, Mr.—"Boz"	Bloomsbury Christening	
Darnay, Charles ...	Tale Of Two Cities, Book 2	2
Dartle, Rosa	David Copperfield	20
Datchery, Mr.	Edwin Drood	18
David	Nicholas Nickleby	37
David	Martin Chuzzlewit	13
David	Old Curiosity Shop	54

Character or place.	*Book.*	*Chap.*
Davis, Mr., Mrs. and party	Pictures From Italy	
Davis, Gill	Perils Of Certain English Prisoners	1
Dawes	Little Dorrit, Book 2	21
Dawkins, Jack	Oliver Twist	8
Dawson, Mr. Surgeon— " Boz "	Our Parish	3
Deaf Gentleman, The	Master Humphrey's Clock	1
Dean, The	Edwin Drood	2
Dedlock, Sir Leicester and Lady	Bleak House	2
Dedlock, Sir Morbury and Lady	Bleak House	7
Dedlock, Volumnia Miss	Bleak House	28
Dedlock, Cousins ...	Bleak House	40
Deedles	The Chimes, 2nd quarter	
Defarge, Monsr. and Madame	Tale Of Two Cities, Book 1	5
Defresnier and Co. ...	No Thoroughfare—Act 1 : New Characters, etc.	
De la Cour, Capitaine	Somebody's Luggage— His Boots	
Denham, Mr.	The Haunted Man	2
Dennis	Barnaby Rudge	36
Dentist's Servant ...	Uncommercial Travel- ler	16
Deputy	Edwin Drood	5

Character or place.	*Book.*	*Chap.*
Derrick, John	Dr. Marigold's Prescriptions	6
Devasseur, Monsr. Loyal	Reprinted Pieces— Our French Watering Place	
Dibbles, The	Uncommercial Traveller	20
Dick	Oliver Twist	7
Dick	Lazy Tour Of Two Idle Apprentices	4
Dick, Mr.	David Copperfield	13
Dilber, Mrs.	Christmas Carol Stave	4
Dingley Dell	Pickwick	4
Dingo, Professor... ...	Bleak House	13
Diogenes	Dombey And Son	14
Dismal Jemmy	Pickwick	3
Diver, Colonel	Martin Chuzzlewit	16
Dixons, The—" Boz "	Mrs. J. Porter	
Dobbles, The—" Boz "	The New Year	
Dobbs, Julia	The Strange Gentleman	
Doctor of Law—" Boz "	Doctors Commons	
Doctor's Servant ...	Uncommercial Traveller	16
Dodson and Fogg ...	Pickwick	18
Do'em	Pantomime Of Life	
Dolloby, Mr.	David Copperfield	13
Dolls, Mr.	Our Mutual Friend, Book 2	2
Dolphin's Head	Uncommercial Traveller	22

Character or place.	*Book.*	*Chap.*
Dombey, Mr. and Mrs., Paul and Florence ...	Dombey And Son	1
Donny Miss	Bleak House	3
Dor, Madame	No Thoroughfare—Act 1 : New Characters, etc.	
Dornton, Sergeant ...	Reprinted Pieces— Detective Police	
Dorrit, Little	Little Dorrit, Book 1	5
Dorrit, William Mr. ...	Little Dorrit, Book 1	6
Dorrit, Edward and Fanny	Little Dorrit, Book 1	7
Dorrit, Frederick ...	Little Dorrit, Book 1	8
Dotheboys Hall	Nicholas Nickleby	3
" Double "	Little Dorrit, Book 1	4
Doubledick, Richard ...	Seven Poor Travellers	1
Dounce, Mr.—" Boz "	Mr. J. Dounce	
Dover Mail	Tale Of Two Cities, Book 1	2
Dowler, Mr. and Mrs.	Pickwick	35
Doyce, Daniel, Mr. ...	Little Dorrit, Book 1	10
Doylance, Old	Haunted House—Ghost in Master B's Room	
Doze, Professor	Mudfog Papers, 1st Meeting	
Drawley, Mr.	Mudfog Papers, 2nd Meeting	
Drooce, Sergeant ...	Perils Of Certain English Prisoners	1
Drood, Edwin	Edwin Drood	2

Character or place.	Book.	Chap.
Drowvey and Grimmer, Misses	Holiday Romance	1
Dringworth, Brothers	Message From The Sea	5
Drummle, Bentley	Great Expectations	23
Drunkard's Death, The—" Boz "	Tales	12
Dubbley	Pickwick	24
Duchess, The	Holiday Romance	2
Duff	Oliver Twist	31
Dulborough Town	Uncommercial Traveller	12
Dull, Mr.	Mudfog Papers, 2nd Meeting	
Dumbledon	Reprinted Pieces— Our School	
Dumkins	Pickwick	7
Dummins, Mr.	Sketches, Young Gents— Out and Out	
Dummy, Mr.	Mudfog Papers, 2nd Meeting	
Dumps, Mr. Nicodemus—" Boz "	Bloomsbury Christening	
Dunday, Dr.	Reprinted Pieces— Detective Police	
Dunkle, Ginery, Dr.	Martin Chuzzlewit	34
Durdles, Stony	Edwin Drood	4

E

| East Indiaman | Reprinted Pieces— Long Voyage | |

Character or place.	*Book.*	*Chap.*
Eatanswill Gazette ...	Pickwick	13
Eatanswill Independent	Pickwick	13
Eden	Martin Chuzzlewit	23
Edith	Dombey And Son	21
Edkins, Mr.—" Boz "	Steam Excursion	
Edmonds, George ...	Village Coquettes	
Edmunds family ...	Pickwick	6
Edson, Mr. and Mrs....	Mrs. Lirriper's Lodgings	1
Edwards, Miss	Old Curiosity Shop	31
Edwin	The Holly Tree Inn—The Guest	
Elizabeth, Miss	Our Mutual Friend, Book 1	5
Emigrants	American Notes	11
Emile	Somebody's Luggage—His Boots	
Emily, Little	David Copperfield	3
Emmeline	Holly Tree Inn—The Bill	
Endell, Martha	David Copperfield	22
Engine, Fire—" Boz "	The Parish	1
Englishman, The ...	Uncommercial Traveller	28
Estella	Great Expectations	8
Eugene	Somebody's Luggage—His Boots	
Eustace, Mr.	Little Dorrit, Book 2	5
Evans, Jemima, her mother and sisters—" Boz "	Miss Evans And The Eagle	

Character or place.	Book.	Chap.
Evans, Mr.—" Boz "	Mrs. J. Porter	
Evenson, Mr.—" Boz "	The Boarding House	2
Evremond, St.	Tale Of Two Cities,	
	Book 2	24
Execution at Rome ...	Pictures From Italy	
Ezekiel	Mugby Junction—	
	Boy at Mugby	

F

Facemaker, The ...	Uncommercial Travel-	
	ler	25
Fagin, Old	Oliver Twist	8
Fairfax, Mr.	Sketches, Young Gents--	
	The Censorious	
Fair Freedom	Reprinted Pieces—	
	Prince Bull	
Family Pet, The ...	Oliver Twist	31
Fan, Little	Christmas Carol Stave 2	
Fang, Mr.	Oliver Twist	11
Fareway family	George Silverman's	
	Explanation	7
Farm, Manor	Pickwick	4
Farmer, General ...	Tale Of Two Cities,	
	Book 2	7
Fat Lady	Nicholas Nickleby	16
Fat Lady	House To Let—	
	Going Into Society	
Father (Young) at Con-		
vent	Little Dorrit, Book 2	1

Character or place.	*Book.*	*Chap.*
Fee, Dr.	Mudfog Papers, 1st Meeting	
Feeder, Mr.	Dombey And Son	11
Feenix, Cousin	Dombey And Son	21
Fendall, Sergeant ...	Reprinted Pieces--- Detective Police	
Fern, Will and Lilian	The Chimes, 2nd quarter	
Feroce, Monsr.	Reprinted Pieces— Our French Watering Place	
Ferrara	Pictures From Italy	
Fezziwig, Old and family	Christmas Carol, Stave 2	
Fibbitson, Mrs.	David Copperfield	5
Fielding, May and Mrs.	Cricket On The Hearth, Chirp 2	
Fielding, Sir John ...	Barnaby Rudge	58
Fielding, Emma ...	Sketches, Young Couples—The Young Couple	
Fiercy, Hon. Capt. Fitzwhisker	Pantomime Of Life	
Fikey	Reprinted Pieces— Detective Police	
Filer, Mr.	The Chimes, 1st quarter	
Filletoville, Marquis of	Pickwick	49
Finches of the Grove	Great Expectations	34
Finching, Mrs.	Sketches, Young Couples—The Plausible	
Finching, Flora	Little Dorrit, Book 1	13
Fipps, Mr.	Martin Chuzzlewit	39

Character or place.	Book.	Chap.
Fish, Mr.	The Chimes, 2nd quarter	
Fisher, Mr. and Mrs....	Perils Of Certain English Prisoners	1
First of May—" Boz "	Scenes	20
Fitzball	Sketches, Young Gents— The Theatrical	
Fitz-Sordust, Colonel ...	Sketches, Young Gents— The Military	
Fitz-Marshall, Mr. ...	Pickwick	15
Five Sisters of York ...	Nicholas Nickleby	6
Fixem—" Boz " ...	Our Parish	5
Fizkin, Horatio	Pickwick	13
Fladdock, General ...	Martin Chuzzlewit	17
Flair, Hon. Augustus— " Boz "	Winglebury Duel	
Flam, Hon. Sparkins	Village Coquettes	
Flamwell, Mr.—" Boz "	Horatio Sparkins	
Flanders family	Uncommercial Traveller	26
Flasher, Mr. Wilkins...	Pickwick	55
Fledgeby, Fascination	Our Mutual Friend, Book, 2	4
Fleet Prison	Pickwick	40
Fleetwoods, The— " Boz "	Steam Excursion	
Fleming, Agnes	Oliver Twist	51
Fletcher, Christian ...	Reprinted Pieces— Long Voyage	
Flimkins, Mr. and Mrs.	Sketches, Young Gents— The Theatrical	

Character or place.	*Book.*	*Chap.*
Flintwinch, Jeremiah and Affery	Little Dorrit, Book 1	3
Flipfield family	Uncommercial Traveller	19
Flite, Miss	Bleak House	3
Flopson	Great Expectations	22
Florence	Pictures From Italy	
Flowers	Dombey And Son	36
Flummery, Mr.	Mudfog Papers, 2nd Meeting	
Fogg, Mr.	Pickwick	18
Fogle Hunter, Mr. ...	Mudfog Papers, 2nd Meeting	
Folair, Mr.	Nicholas Nickleby	23
Force, La	Tale of Two Cities, Book 1	3
Fort, Spirit of the ...	Uncommercial Traveller	24
Foulon	Tale of Two Cities, Book 2	22
Foundling Hospital ...	No Thoroughfare— The Overture	
Foxey, Old	Old Curiosity Shop	36
Foxey, Dr.	Mudfog Papers, 2nd Meeting	
Frank, Little	Reprinted Pieces— Poor Relation's Story	
French Flemish Country	Uncommercial Traveller	25
French Courier	Pictures From Italy	

Character or place.	*Book.*	*Chap.*
French Gentleman, from the Consul ...	Mrs. Lirriper's Legacy	1
French Officer	Seven Poor Travellers	1
Frithers, Mr.	Sketches, Young Couples—The Plausible	
Frost, Miss	Reprinted Pieces— Our School	

G

" G "	Tom Tiddler's Ground	6
Gabelle	Tale Of Two Cities, Book 2	8
Game Chicken	Dombey And Son	22
Gamfield	Oliver Twist	3
Gamp, Mrs.	Martin Chuzzlewit	19
Gander, Mr.	Martin Chuzzlewit	9
Gaoler and Child ...	Little Dorrit, Book 1	1
Gardens—" Boz " ...	London Recreations	
Gargery, Joe and Mrs.	Great Expectations	1
Garland, Mr. and Mrs.	Old Curiosity Shop	14
Garland, Mr. Abel ...	Old Curiosity Shop	14
Garraways	Uncommercial Traveller	21
Gashford, Mr.	Barnaby Rudge	35
Gaspard	Tale of Two Cities, Book 1	5
Gattletons, The— " Boz "	Mrs. J. Porter	
Gay, Walter	Dombey And Son	4
Gazings, Miss	Nicholas Nickleby	23

Character or place.	Book.	Chap.
General Agency Office	Nicholas Nickleby	16
General, Mrs.	Little Dorrit, Book 2	1
Genoa	Pictures From Italy	
Gentleman, Foreign, The	Our Mutual Friend, Book 1	11
Gentleman, Old	Cricket On The Hearth	Chirp 1
George, Mrs.	Old Curiosity Shop	4
George, carman	Old Curiosity Shop	26
George, Mr.	Bleak House	21
George, Master	Our Mutual Friend Book 1	5
George	Nicholas Nickleby	14
George and Vulture ...	Pickwick	26
Ghastly Grim, Saint	Uncommercial Traveller	21
Gilbert, Mark	Barnaby Rudge	8
Giles	Oliver Twist	28
Gills, Solomon	Dombey And Son	4
Gimblet, Brother ...	George Silverman's Explanation	6
Gin Shops—"Boz"	Scenes	22
Glamour, Bob	Our Mutual Friend, Book 1	6
Glibbery, Bob	Our Mutual Friend, Book 1	6
Globson	Uncommercial Traveller	19
Glogwood, Sir Chipkins	Sketches, Young Couples—The Egotistical	

Character or place.	Book.	Chap.
Glorious Apollers ...	Old Curiosity Shop	13
Glubb, Old	Dombey And Son	12
Glumper, Sir Thomas—		
" Boz "	Mrs. J. Porter	
Goat and Boots, The—		
" Boz "	Our Parish	2
Gobler, Mr.—" Boz "	The Boarding House	2
Gog and Magog	Master Humphrey's	
Chronicles	Clock	1
Goggle-eyed Gent ...	Haunted House—Mortals	
	In The House	
Goldstraw, Mrs.	No Thoroughfare—Act	
	1 : Enter the House-	
	keeper	
Golden Cross	David Copperfield	19
Golden Square	Nicholas Nickleby	2
Goodchild, Francis ...	Lazy Tour Of Two Idle	
	Apprentices	1
Good Republican ...	Tale of Two Cities,	
	Book 3	8
Goodwin	Pickwick	18
Gordon, Lord George	Barnaby Rudge	35
Gordon, Colonel ...	Barnaby Rudge	49
Goswell Street	Pickwick	2
Government Officer ...	Hard Times, Book 1	2
Governor, Jack	Haunted House—Mortals	
	In The House	
Gowan, Henry	Little Dorrit, Book 1	17
Gowan, Mrs.	Little Dorrit, Book 1	26
Gracchi, Modern, The	Martin Chuzzlewit	22

Character or place.	Book.	Chap.
Gradgrind, Thomas ...	Hard Times, Book 1	2
Gradgrind, Louisa and Tom	Hard Times, Book 1	3
Gradgrind, Mrs. and younger children ...	Hard Times, Book 1	4
Graham, Mary	Martin Chuzzlewit	3
Graham, Hugh	Master Humphrey's Clock	1
Grainger	David Copperfield	24
Granby, Marquis of ...	Pickwick	27
Grandfather, Nell's ...	Old Curiosity Shop	1
Grandmarina	Holiday Romance	2
Grand Vizier	Haunted House—Ghost In Master B.'s Room	
Granger, Mrs.	Dombey And Son	21
Grannett	Oliver Twist	23
Granville, Wharton ...	George Silverman's Explanation	9
Graymarsh	Nicholas Nickleby	8
Grayper, Mrs.	David Copperfield	2
Grazinlands, Mr. and Mrs.	Uncommercial Traveller	6
Great Tasmania's Cargo	Uncommercial Traveller	8
Great White Horse, Ipswich	Pickwick	22
Gregsbury, Mr.	Nicholas Nickleby	16
Green, Mr.—" Boz "	Vauxhall Gardens	
Green, Tom	Barnaby Rudge	58
Greengrocer, Dulborough	Uncommercial Traveller	12

Character or place.	Book.	Chap.
Greenwich Fair—" Boz "	Scenes	12
Greenwich Pensioners	Uncommercial Traveller	27
Greenwood, Miss ...	Sketches, Young Gents— The Censorious	
Gregory	David Copperfield	11
Greta Bridge	Nicholas Nickleby	6
Grewgious, Mr.	Edwin Drood	9
Grey, The Misses ...	Sketches, Young Gents— The Domestic	
Gride, Arthur	Nicholas Nickleby	47
Gridley	Bleak House	15
Griffin	Haunted House— Ghost in Master B.'s Room	
Grig, Tom	The Lamplighter	
Griggins, Mr.	Sketches, Young Gents— The Funny	
Grime, Professor ...	Mudfog Papers, 2nd Meeting	
Grimmer, Miss	Holiday Romance	1
Grimwig, Mr.	Oliver Twist	14
Grimwood, Eliza ...	Reprinted Pieces— Detective Anecdotes	
Grinder	Old Curiosity Shop	17
Grip, The Raven ...	Barnaby Rudge	6
Groves, James	Old Curiosity Shop	29
Grompus	Our Mutual Friend, Book 1	11
Groper, Colonel	Martin Chuzzlewit	34
Grub, Gabriel and the Goblin	Pickwick	29

Character or place.	*Book.*	*Chap.*
Grub, Mr.	Mudfog Papers, 2nd Meeting	
Grubble, W.	Bleak House	37
Grudden, Mrs.	Nicholas Nickleby	23
Grueby, John	Barnaby Rudge	35
Gruff and Glum	Our Mutual Friend, Book 4	4
Gruff and Tackleton ...	Cricket On The Hearth Chirp	1
Grummidge, Dr. ...	Mudfog Papers, 2nd Meeting	
Grummer	Pickwick	24
Guard, Dover Mail ...	Tale Of Two Cities, Book 1	2
Guard	Mugby Junction	1
Gubbins, Mr.—" Boz "	Our Parish	2
Gubbinses, The— " Boz "	Mrs. J. Porter	
Guests at Dinner Party	Dombey And Son	36
Gulpidge, Mr. and Mrs.	David Copperfield	25
Gummidge, Mrs. ...	David Copperfield	3
Gunter, Mr.	Pickwick	32
Guppy, Mr.	Bleak House	4
Guppy, Mrs.	Bleak House	38
Gusher, Mr.	Bleak House	8
Guster	Bleak House	10

H

Hackney Coach Stands— " Boz "	Scenes	7

Character or place.	Book.	Chap.
Haggage, Dr.	Little Dorrit, Book 1	6
Half-pay Captain—		
" Boz "	Our Parish	2
Halsewell, The	Reprinted Pieces—	
	Long Voyage	
Hamlet's Aunt	David Copperfield	25
Hampton Court	Little Dorrit, Book 1	26
Handbell Ringer—		
" Boz "	Doctors Commons	
Handel, (Pip)	Great Expectations	22
Handford, Julius ...	Our Mutual Friend,	
	Book 1	3
Hardy, Mr.—" Boz "	Steam Excursion	
Haredale, Mr.	Barnaby Rudge	1
Haredale, Emma ...	Barnaby Rudge	1
Harker, Mr.	Dr. Marigold's Pre-	
	scription	6
Harleigh, Mr.—" Boz "	Mrs. J. Porter	
Harley Street	Little Dorrit, Book 1	20
Harmon, John	Our Mutual Friend,	
	Book 1	2
Harris	Old Curiosity Shop	16
Harris, Mr.—" Boz "	Mr. J. Dounce	
Harris, Mrs.	Martin Chuzzlewit	19
Harrisburgh	American Notes	9
Harry, Little	Old Curiosity Shop	25
Hart, Mr.	American Notes	3
Hartford	American Notes	5
Harthouse, Mr. James	Hard Times, Book 2	2

Character or place.	*Book.*	*Chap.*
Harveys, The	Sketches, Young Couples—The Young and Old Couple	
Hatter, The	Uncommercial Traveller	16
Havisham, Miss ...	Great Expectations	8
Havisham, Arthur ...	Great Expectations	42
Hawdon, Captain ...	Bleak House	26
Hawk, Sir Mulberry ...	Nicholas Nickleby	19
Hawkyard, Brother ...	George Silverman's Explanation	4
Head, Saracen's The Towcester	Pickwick	51
Head, Saracen's The, Snow Hill	Nicholas Nickleby	3
Headstone, Bradley ...	Our Mutual Friend, Book 2	1
Heathfield, Alfred ...	Battle Of Life	1
Heep, Uriah	David Copperfield	15
Heep, Mrs.	David Copperfield	17
Helves,Captain—"Boz"	Steam Excursion	
Henrietta	Somebody's Luggage—Brown Paper Parcel	
Henry, Mr.—" Boz "	Pawnbroker's Shop	
Herbert, Mr.	Barnaby Rudge	73
Herculaneum	Pictures From Italy	
Hermitage	Pictures From Italy	
Herschell, John	Haunted House—Mortals In The House	
Hexham, Gaffer and Lizzie	Our Mutual Friend, Book 1	1

8

Character or place.	Book.	Chap.
Hexham, Charley ...	Our Mutual Friend, Book 1	3
Heyling family	Pickwick	21
Hicks, Mr. Septimus— " Boz "	The Boarding House	1
Hicksons, The—" Boz "	Mrs. J. Porter	
Higden, Betty	Our Mutual Friend, Book 1	16
Hilton, Mr.—" Boz "	Sentiment	
Hoghton Towers ...	George Silverman's Explanation	4
Holliday, Arthur ...	Lazy Tour Of Two Idle Apprentices	2
Holy Staircase	Pictures From Italy	
Holy Week	Pictures From Italy	
Hominy, Mrs.	Martin Chuzzlewit	22
Honeythunder, Mr. ...	Edwin Drood	6
Hookem, Snivey, Sir	Mudfog Papers, 2nd Meeting	
Hopkins—" Boz " ...	Our Parish	4
Hopkins, Captain ...	David Copperfield	11
Hopkins, Mr.	Sketches, Young Gents— The Bashful	
Hopkins, Jack	Pickwick	32
Horse Guards	Little Dorrit, Book 1	21
Horse Guards	Barnaby Rudge	49
Horse, Great White, Ipswich	Pickwick	22
Hortense, Mlle.	Bleak House	12
Hospitals, Boston ...	American Notes	3

Character or place.	*Book.*	*Chap.*
Hospital Patient, The—		
"Boz"	Characters	6
Hôtel, de l' Ecu d' Or ...	Pictures From Italy	
Housemaid at Maylie's	Oliver Twist	28
Houses of Reformation		
and Correction ...	American Notes	3
Houses of Represen-		
tatives	American Notes	8
Howe, Dr.	American Notes	3
Howler, Rev. Melchise-		
deck	Dombey And Son	15
Hubble, Mr. and Mrs.	Great Expectations	4
Hugh of the Maypole	Barnaby Rudge	10
Hughes, The Revs. ...	Uncommercial Travel-	
	ler	2
Humm, Mr. Anthony	Pickwick	33
Humpbacked Man ...	Oliver Twist	32
Hunter, Horace—		
"Boz"	Winglebury Duel	
Hunter, Leo, Mr. and		
Mrs.	Pickwick	15
Hunt and Wilkins ...	Pickwick	19
Husband (Betsy Trot-		
wood's)	David Copperfield	47
Hypolite (Private) ...	Somebody's Luggage—	
	His Boots	

I

Idle, Mr. Thomas ...	Lazy Tour Of Two Idle	
	Apprentices	1

Character or place.	*Book.*	*Chap.*
" Ikey "	Haunted House—Mortals In The House	
Ikey—" Boz "	Watkins Tottle	2
Indian, The	House To Let—Going Into Society	
Indian Savage	Nicholas Nickleby	23
Innkeeper at Martigny	Little Dorrit, Book 2	3
Innkeeper	Lazy Tour Of Two Idle Apprentices	1
Inspector, Mr.	Our Mutual Friend, Book 1	3
Irish Pedlar—" Boz "	Our Parish	6
Ironworker	Old Curiosity Shop	44
Isaac	Pickwick	46
Italian Prisoner	Uncommercial Traveller	28
Izzard, Mr.	Martin Chuzzlewit	34

J

Jackman, Major	Mrs. Lirriper's Lodgings	1
Jackson	Pickwick	20
Jackson, Mr. and Mrs.	Sketches, Young Couples—The Plausible	
Jackson, Mr. Young ...	Mugby Junction—Barbox Brothers	
Jacob (Little)	Old Curiosity Shop	13
Jacobs, Solomon " Boz "	Mr. Watkins Tottle	2

Character or place.	*Book.*	*Chap.*
Jacques, The Three ...	Tale Of Two Cities, Book 1	5
Jaggers, Mr.	Great Expectations	18
Jaggers' Housekeeper	Great Expectations	26
Jailers	Oliver Twist	52
Jairings Hotel	Uncommercial Traveller	6
James—" Boz " ...	The Boarding House	1
James and Charlotte ...	Sketches, Young Couples—The Contradictory	
Jane—" Boz "	" The House "	
Jane, Aunt	Our Mutual Friend, Book 1	5
Janet	David Copperfield	13
Jarley, Mrs.	Old Curiosity Shop	26
Jarndyce	Bleak House	1
Jarndyce, Tom	Bleak House	1
Jarndyce, John	Bleak House	3
Jarvis	No Thoroughfare—Act 1 : Enter the Housekeeper	
Jasper, Mr.	Edwin Drood	2
Jeddler, Dr., Grace and Marion	Battle Of Life	1
Jellyby, Mr. and Mrs.	Bleak House	4
Jellyby, Caddy, Peepy, etc.	Bleak House	4
Jemmy, Dismal	Pickwick	3
Jemmy	Mrs. Lirriper's Lodgings	1

Character or place.	Book.	Chap.
Jenkins, Mr.—" Boz "	Mrs. J. Porter	
Jenkins, Mr.	Sketches, Young Couples—The Contradictory	
Jennings, Mr.	Mudfog Papers—Life of Mr. Tulrumble	
Jennings, Rodolph, Mr. and Mrs.—" Boz "	The Mistaken Milliner	
Jennings, Mr.—" Boz "	Mr. J. Dounce	
Jenny	Bleak House	8
Jerry	Old Curiosity Shop	18
Jerry ... ..., ...	Tale Of Two Cities, Book 1	2
Jesuit, The	Pictures From Italy	
Jilkins, Mr.	Reprinted Pieces— " Our Bore ".	
Jingle, Alfred	Pickwick	2
Jiniwin, Mrs.	Old Curiosity Shop	4
Jinks ... ., ...	Pickwick	24
Jinkins	Pickwick	14
Jinkins—" Boz " ...	Pawnbroker's Shop	
Jinkins, Mr.	Martin Chuzzlewit	9
Jinkinson	Master Humphrey's Clock	5
Jip	David Copperfield	26
Jobba, Mr.	Mudfog Papers, 1st Meeting	
Jobbling, Dr.	Martin Chuzzlewit	27
Jobbling	Bleak House	20
Jobsons, The	Uncommercial Traveller	20

Character or place.	Book.	Chap.
Jock	Lazy Tour Of Two Idle Apprentices	2
Jodd, Mr.	Martin Chuzzlewit	34
Jo, Poor	Bleak House	11
Joe, Fat Boy	Pickwick	4
Joe, Old	Christmas Carol, Stave 4	
Joe	Tale Of Two Cities, Book 1	2
John, Mr.	Sketches, Young Couples —The Young Couple	
John	Reprinted Pieces— Poor Relations Story	
John	Haunted House—Mortals In The House	
John, Old	Reprinted Pieces— Poor Man's Tale Of A Patent	
Johnson	Dombey And Son	12
Johnson, Mr.	Nicholas Nickleby	16
Johnson, John	The Strange Gentleman	
Johnson Parkers—"Boz"	Our Parish	6
Jolly Sandboys	Old Curiosity Shop	18
Jolly Boatmen	Mudfog Papers—Life of Mr. Tulrumble	
Jolly Fellowship Porters	Our Mutual Friend, Book 1	6
Jolterhed, Sir W. ...	Mudfog Papers, 2nd Meeting	
Jonathan	Our Mutual Friend, Book 1	6

Character or place.		*Book.*	*Chap.*
Jones, Mr.—" Boz "		Mr. Minns And His Cousin	
Jones—" Boz "		Mr. J. Dounce	
Joram		David Copperfield	9
Jorgan, Capt.		Message From The Sea	1
Jorkins, Mr.		David Copperfield	23
Joseph and Celia ...		Uncommercial Traveller	21
Joseph		Somebody's Luggage—Leaving It Till Called For	
Jowl		Old Curiosity Shop	42
Joy, Thomas		Reprinted Pieces—Poor Man's Tale Of A Patent	
Judge, The—" Boz "		Doctors Commons	
Judge, Old Bailey ...		Tale of Two Cities, Book 2	2
Judge and Jury		Dr. Marigold's Prescriptions	6
Jupe, Sissy		Hard Times, Book 1	2
Jupe, Signor		Hard Times, Book 1	3

K

Kags		Oliver Twist	50
Kate the Orphan		Dombey And Son	24
Kedgick, Capt.		Martin Chuzzlewit	22
Kenge, Mr.		Bleak House	3
Kentucky Giant ...		American Notes	12
Kenwigs family		Nicholas Nickleby	14

Character or place.	Book.	Chap.
Ketch, Professor ...	Mudfog Papers, 2nd Meeting	
Kettle, La Fayette, Mr.	Martin Chuzzlewit	21
Kibble, Jacob	Our Mutual Friend, Book 1	3
Kidderminster, Master	Hard Times, Book 1	6
Kimmeens, Miss ...	Tom Tiddler's Ground	6
Kindheart, Mr.	Uncommercial Traveller	26
King, C. G.	Perils Of Certain English Prisoners	1
King of Bill Stickers	Reprinted Pieces— Bill-sticking	
Kit	Old Curiosity Shop	1
Kitten, Mr.	Perils Of Certain English Prisoners	1
Kitterbell, Mr. and Mrs.—" Boz " ...	Bloomsbury Christening	
Kitty	Message From The Sea	1
Klem Family, The ...	Uncommercial Traveller	16
Knag, Miss	Nicholas Nickleby	10
Knag, Mortimer, Mr.	Nicholas Nickleby	18
Knight Bell, Dr. ...	Mudfog Papers, 1st Meeting	
Krook	Bleak House	5
Kutankumagen, Dr.	Mudfog Papers, 1st Meeting	
Kwakley, Mr.	Mudfog Papers, 2nd Meeting	

L

Character or place.	*Book.*	*Chap.*
Ladle, Joey	No Thoroughfare— Act 1 : The Curtain Rises	1
" Lady Jane "	Bleak House	5
Lagnier, Monsieur ...	Little Dorrit, Book 1	11
Lake Steamboats ...	American Notes	15
Lambert, Mr.	Sketches, Young Gents— The Bashful	
Lame Man, The ...	Pickwick	40
Lammle Alfred	Our Mutual Friend, Book 1	10
Lamps	Mugby Junction— Barbox Bros.	
Llanallgo	Uncommercial Travel- ler	2
Landless, Neville ...	Edwin Drood	6
Landless, Helena ...	Edwin Drood	6
Landlord Three Cripples	Oliver Twist	26
Landlord Peal of Bells	Tom Tiddler's Ground	1
Landlord at Inn ...	Haunted House—Mortals In The House	
Landlord and Lady	Lazy Tour Of Two Idle Apprentices	2
Langdale, Mr.	Barnaby Rudge	61
Langley	Somebody's Luggage— His Boots	
Larkins, Mr. and Miss	David Copperfield	18
Lascar, The	Edwin Drood	1

Character or place.	Book.	Chap.
Leath, Angela	Holly Tree Inn—The Guest	
Leather Bottle, Cobham	Pickwick	11
Leaver, Mr. and Mrs.	Sketches, Young Couples—The Loving	
Leaver and Scroo, Messrs.	Mudfog Papers, 2nd Meeting	
Ledbrain, Mr.	Mudfog Papers, 1st Meeting	
Ledbrook, Miss ...	Nicholas Nickleby	23
Leeford, Edward ...	Oliver Twist	49
Lemon, Mrs.	Holiday Romance	4
Lenville, Mr. and Mrs.	Nicholas Nickleby	23
Lewsome, Mr.	Martin Chuzzlewit	29
Lighterman's Arms ...	Mudfog Papers—Life of Mr. Tulrumble	
Lightwood, Mortimer	Our Mutual Friend, Book 1	2
Lillerton, Miss— "Boz"	Watkins Tottle	1
Lillyvick, Mr.	Nicholas Nickleby	14
Limbkins, Mr.	Oliver Twist	2
Limbury, Mr. and Mrs.	Is She His Wife?	
Lillian	The Chimes, 2nd quarter	
Linderwood, Lieutenant	Perils Of Certain English Prisoners—The Island	
Linkinwater, Tom . .	Nicholas Nickleby	35
Linkinwater's, Tom, sister	Nicholas Nickleby	37
"Lion"	Little Dorrit, Book 1	17

Character or place.	*Book.*	*Chap.*
Lion A, Some Particulars Concerning	Mudfog Papers	
Lirriper, Mrs.	Mrs. Lirriper's Lodgings and Legacy	
Lirriper, Joshua ...	Mrs. Lirriper's Legacy	1
List, Isaac	Old Curiosity Shop	29
Liston, Mr.	Sketches, Young Gents— The Theatrical	
Littimer	David Copperfield	21
Little Bethel	Old Curiosity Shop	41
Lively, Mr.	Oliver Twist	26
Liverpool Workhouse	Uncommercial Traveller	8
" Liz "	Bleak House	31
Lobbs, Old and Maria	Pickwick	17
Lobley	Edwin Drood	22
Lobskini, Signor— " Boz "	Sentiment	
Loggins, Mr.—" Boz "	Steam Excursion	
London, Arcadian ...	Uncommercial Traveller	16
Longford, Edmund ...	Haunted Man	2
Long Eers, Hon. and Rev.	Mudfog Papers, 2nd Meeting	
Long-legged Young Man	David Copperfield	12
Longlost	Uncommercial Traveller	19
Looking Glass Prairie	American Notes	13
Lord Warden Hotel ...	Uncommercial Traveller	17

Character or place.	Book.	Chap.
Lord Mayor	Barnaby Rudge	61
Lord Chamberlain ...	Holiday Romance	2
Lorn, Mr.	Lazy Tour Of Two Idle Apprentices	2
Lorry, Mr. Jarvis ...	Tale Of Two Cities, Book 1	2
Losberne, Dr.	Oliver Twist	29
Lotteries	Pictures From Italy	
Louisville	American Notes	12
Lowten, Mr.	Pickwick	20
Lovetown, Mr. and Mrs.	Is She His Wife?	
Lowfield, Miss	Sketches, Young Gents— The Poetical	
Lucas, Sol	Pickwick	15
Lucie, Little	Tale Of Two Cities, Book 2	21
Luffey	Pickwick	7
Lumbey, Dr.	Nicholas Nickleby	36
Lummy, Ned	Martin Chuzzlewit	13
Lupin, Mrs.	Martin Chuzzlewit	8
Linx, Miss	Tom Tiddler's Ground	6
Lying Awake	Reprinted Pieces	

M

Macey, Mr. and Mrs.	Perils Of Certain English Prisoners— The Island	1
Mackin, Mrs.—" Boz "	Pawnbroker's Shop	
Macklin, Mrs.—" Boz "	Streets by Night	

Character or place.	Book.	Chap.
Macmanus, Mr.	Reprinted Pieces— Long Voyage	
Macstinger, Mrs. ...	Dombey And Son	9
Macstinger, Alexander	Dombey And Son	23
Macstinger, Juliana ...	Dombey And Son	25
Mad Gentleman, The	Nicholas Nickleby	41
Madgers, Winifred ...	Mrs. Lirriper's Legacy	1
Madman's Story	Pickwick	11
Maddox, John	Village Coquettes	
Magg, Mr.	Reprinted Pieces— Our Vestry	
Maggy	Little Dorrit, Book 1	9
Magistrates	Oliver Twist	3
Magnates	Little Dorrit, Book 1	21
Magnus, Mr. Peter ...	Pickwick	22
Magpie and Stump ...	Pickwick	20
Magsman, Toby ...	House To Let—Going Into Society	
Magwitch	Great Expectations	40
Maldon, Jack	David Copperfield	16
Maldertons, The—		
"Boz"	Horatio Sparkins	
Mallard, Mr.	Pickwick	31
Mallett, Mr.	Mudfog Papers, 2nd Meeting	
Mamertine Prisons ...	Pictures From Italy	
Man in Monument ...	Martin Chuzzlewit	37
Manette, Dr.	Tale Of Two Cities, Book 1	5
Manette, Miss	Tale Of Two Cities, Book 1	4

Character or place.	*Book.*	*Chap.*
Mann, Mrs.	Oliver Twist	2
Manners, Julia—		
" Boz "	Winglebury Duel	
Mansel, Miss	Reprinted Pieces— Long Voyage	
Mansfield, Lord and Lady	Barnaby Rudge	66
Mantalini, Madame and Monsr.	Nicholas Nickleby	10
Mantalini's customers	Nicholas Nickleby	18
Mantua	Pictures From Italy	
Maplesones—" Boz "	The Boarding House	1
Marchioness, The ...	Old Curiosity Shop	36
Marguerite	No Thoroughfare— Act 1 : New Characters	
Marigold, Dr.	Dr. Marigold's Prescriptions	
Markham	David Copperfield	24
Markleham, Mrs. ...	David Copperfield	16
Marks, Will	Master Humphrey's Clock	3
Marley, Jacob and Ghost	Christmas Carol	1
Marquis, The	Tale Of Two Cities, Book 2	7
Maroon, Captain ...	Little Dorrit, Book 1	12
Marseilles Prison	Little Dorrit, Book 1	1
Marshal, The	Little Dorrit, Book 1	36
Marshall, Miss	Sketches, Young Gents— The Censorious	
Marshall, Mary ...	Seven Poor Travellers	1

Character or place.	*Book.*	*Chap.*
Marshalsea Prison ...	Little Dorrit, Book 1	6
Martha the Cripple ...	Dombey And Son	24
Martha	Oliver Twist	24
Martha Endell	David Copperfield	22
Martigny Hotel	Little Dorrit, Book 2	3
Martin, Jack	Pickwick	49
Martin, groom	Pickwick	48
Martin, gamekeeper ...	Pickwick	19
Martin, Fleet prisoner	Pickwick	42
Martin, Amelia—"Boz"	The Mistaken Milliner	
Martin, Betsy	The Lamplighter	
Martin, Miss	Somebody's Luggage— Leaving It Till Called For	
Martins, The	Sketches, Young Gents-- The Very Friendly	
Marton, Mr.	Old Curiosity Shop	52
Marwood, Alice	Dombey And Son	34
" Mary "	Pickwick	25
Mary Anne	Our Mutual Friend, Book 2	1
Maryon, Capt. and Miss	Perils Of Certain English Prisoners	1
Mask, The	Master Humphrey's Clock	3
Matinters	Pickwick	35
Matron, The	Seven Poor Travellers	1
Mawls, Master	Reprinted Pieces— Our School	
Maxby	Reprinted Pieces— Our School	

Character or place.	Book.	Chap.
Maxey, Caroline	Mrs. Lirriper's Lodgings	1
May day	Uncommercial Travel-ler	19
Maylie, Mrs. and Rose	Oliver Twist	29
Maylie, Harry	Oliver Twist	34
Mayor of Winglebury—"Boz"	Winglebury Duel	
Mayor of Margate ...	Holiday Romance	3
Maypole Inn, Chigwell	Barnaby Rudge	1
M'Choakumchild, Mr.	Hard Times, Book 1	2
M'Choakumchild, Mrs.	Hard Times, Book 1	9
Meagles, Mr., Mrs. and Minnie	Little Dorrit, Book 1	2
Mealy Potatoes	David Copperfield	11
Mechanics' Institutes	Uncommercial Travel-ler	12
Medical Student ...	Lazy Tour Of Two Idle Apprentices	2
Medicine Men	Uncommercial Travel-ler	26
Meditations In Mon-mouth Street—"Boz"	Scenes	6
Medusa	Our Mutual Friend, Book 1	10
Meek, Mr. and Mrs.	Reprinted Pieces—Births	
Meg	The Chimes, 1st quarter	
Melia	Dombey And Son	12
Mell, Mr.	David Copperfield	5
Mellows, J.	Uncommercial Travel-ler	22

9

Character or place.	*Book.*	*Chap.*
Meltham, Mr.	Hunted Down	1
Melluka	Mugby Junction—Barbox Bros. and Co.	
Melvilleson, Miss ...	Bleak House	32
Mender of Roads ...	Tale Of Two Cities, Book 2	8
Mercantile Jack	Uncommercial Traveller	5
Merdle, Mrs.	Little Dorrit, Book 1	20
Merdle, Mr.	Little Dorrit, Book 1	21
Meriton, Mr.	Reprinted Pieces—Long Voyage	
Merrylegs	Hard Times, Book 1	3
Merriwinkle, Mr. and Mrs.	Sketches, Young Couples—Couple Who Coddle Themselves	
Mescheck	Reprinted Pieces—Detective Police	
Messenger Steamboat	American Notes	11
Mesrour	Haunted House—Ghost In Master B.'s Room	
Metropolitan, etc., Muffin Company ...	Nicholas Nickleby	2
Mews Street, Grosvenor Square	Little Dorrit, Book 1	10
Micawber, Mr., Mrs. and family	David Copperfield	11
Michael	Reprinted Pieces—Poor Relation's Story	
Miff, Mrs.	Dombey And Son	31
Miggs, Miss	Barnaby Rudge	7

Character or place.	*Book.*	*Chap.*
Miggot, Mrs.	Uncommercial Traveller	14
Milan	Pictures From Italy	
Miles Owen, Mr. ...	Master Humphrey's Clock	2
Milkwash, John	Sketches, Young Gents— The Poetical	
Miller, Mr.	Pickwick	6
Millers	Great Expectations	22
Military Character, The	Mrs. Lirriper's Legacy	1
Mills, Julia and Mr. ...	David Copperfield	33
Mills, Miss J.	Reprinted Pieces— Our English Watering Place	
Mills at Lowell	American Notes	4
Milvey, Rev. Frank and Mrs.	Our Mutual Friend, Book 1	9
Mim	Dr. Marigold's Prescriptions	1
Minns, Mr.—" Boz "	Mr. Minns And His Cousin	
Mincin, Mr.	Sketches, Young Gents— The Very Friendly	
Mississippi River ...	American Notes	12
" Missis, Our "	Mugby Junction—Boy at Mugby	
Mistress, The	Somebody's Luggage— Leaving It Till Called For	
Misty, Messrs.	Mudfog Papers, 2nd Meeting	

Character or place.	Book.	Chap.
Mith, Sergeant	Reprinted Pieces— Detective Police	
Mitts, Mrs.	Uncommercial Travel· ler	27
Mivins	Pickwick	41
Mobbs	Nicholas Nickleby	8
Moddle, Augustus ...	Martin Chuzzlewit	32
Model, The	Reprinted Pieces— Ghost Of Art	
Modena	Pictures From Italy	
Monastery, The	Pictures From Italy	
Monks	Oliver Twist	26
Monseigneur	Tale of Two Cities, Book 2	7
Montague, Miss Julia— "Boz"	The Mistaken Milliner	
Montflathers, Miss ...	Old Curiosity Shop	29
Montreal	American Notes	15
Moon	Reprinted Pieces— Our Bore	
Mooney, Mr.	The Lamplighter	
Mopes, Mr.	Tom Tiddler's Ground	1
Morfin, Mr.	Dombey And Son	4
Morgan	Sketches, Young Couples—The Contra- dictory	
Morgue, The	Uncommercial Travel· ler	7 and 18
Mormon Agent	Uncommercial Travel- ler	20
Mould, Mr.	Martin Chuzzlewit	19

Character or place.	*Book.*	*Chap.*
Mould, Mrs. and the Misses	Martin Chuzzlewit	25
Mowcher, Miss	David Copperfield	22
Muddlebranes, Mr. ...	Mudfog Papers, 2nd Meeting	
Mudge, Jonas	Pickwick	33
Muff, Professor	Mudfog Papers, 1st Meeting	
Muggleton	Pickwick	7
Muggs, Sir Alfred— " Boz "	Sentiment	
Mullins, Jack	Our Mutual Friend, Book 1	6
Mullion, John	Wreck of The Golden Mary—The Wreck	
Mullit, Professor ...	Martin Chuzzlewit	16
Murderer, The	Dr. Marigold's Prescriptions	6
Murderer, Capt. ...	Uncommercial Traveller	15
Murgatroyd, Mr ...	Mr. Robert Bolton	
Murdstone, Mr.	David Copperfield	2
Murdstone, Miss ...	David Copperfield	4
Murdstone and Grinby	David Copperfield	10
Museum	Pictures From Italy	
Mutanhed, Lord	Pickwick	35
Mutuel, M.	Somebody's Luggage— His Boots	
Muzzle	Pickwick	24

N

Character or place.	*Book.*	*Chap.*
Nadgett	Martin Chuzzlewit	27
Namby	Pickwick	40
Namelesston	Uncommercial Travel- ler	32
Nancy	Oliver Twist	9
Nandy, Old	Little Dorrit, Book 1	31
Naples	Pictures From Italy	
National Hotel	Martin Chuzzlewit	34
Native, The	Dombey And Son	7
Neckitt family	Bleak House	15
Neeshawts, Dr.	Mudfog Papers, 1st Meeting	
Neighbourhoods, Shy	Uncommercial Travel- ler	10
Nell, Little	Old Curiosity Shop	1
Nemo	Bleak House	5
Nettingall, Misses ...	David Copperfield	18
Newcome, Clemency	Battle of Life	1
New Haven	American Notes	5
New Thermopylae ...	Martin Chuzzlewit	23
New York	American Notes	6
New York Paper Boys	Martin Chuzzlewit	16
Niagara	American Notes	14
Nice	Pictures From Italy	
Nicholas—" Boz " ...	The House	
Nickleby, Godfrey and family	Nicholas Nickleby	1
Nickleby, Ralph ...	Nicholas Nickleby	1

Character cr place.	*Book.*	*Chap.*
Nickleby, Mrs., Kate and Nicholas ...	Nicholas Nickleby	3
Night Walks	Uncommercial Traveller	13
Niner, Margaret	Hunted Down	4
Nipper, Susan	Dombey And Son	3
Nixon, Mr. Felix ...	Sketches, Young Gents—The Domestic	
Nixons, The—" Boz "	Mrs. J. Porter	
Noakes, Percy—" Boz "	The Steam Excursion	
Noakes and Styles, Messrs.	Mudfog Papers, 2nd Meeting	
Noakes, Mrs.	The Strange Gentleman	
Nockemorf	Pickwick	38
Nobody's Story	Reprinted Pieces	
Noddy	Pickwick	32
Noggs, Newman ...	Nicholas Nickleby	2
Nogo, Professor ...	Mudfog Papers, 1st Meeting	
Norah	Holly Tree Inn—Boots	
Normandy	House To Let—Going Into Society	
Norris, Mr.	Martin Chuzzlewit	17
Norton, Squire	Village Coquettes	
Nubbles, Mrs.	Old Curiosity Shop	10
Nuns House	Edwin Drood	3
Nupkins, George, Esq.	Pickwick	24
Nupkins, Mrs. and Miss	Pickwick	25
Nurse's Stories	Uncommercial Traveller	15

O

Character or place.	*Book.*	*Chap.*
Oakum Head	Uncommercial Travel-	
	ler	3
Obenrezier, Jules ...	No Thoroughfare—	
	Act 1 : New Charac-	
	ters, etc.	
O'Bleary, Frederick—		
" Boz "	The Boarding House	2
Odd Girl, The	Haunted House—Mortals	
	In The House	
Officers—" Boz " ...	The House	
Old Bailey, The ...	Tale of Two Cities,	
	Book 2	2
Old Boys—" Boz " ...	Mr. John Dounce	
Old Foxey	Old Curiosity Shop	36
Old Gent—" Boz " ...	Scenes	9
Old Lady—" Boz " ...	Our Parish	2
Old Sally	Oliver Twist	24
Old Soldier, The ...	David Copperfield	16
Old Woman	Edwin Drood	1
Oliver's Mother	Oliver Twist	1
Omer, Mr. and Minnie	David Copperfield	9
Omnibuses—" Boz "	Scenes	16
Orfling, The (Clickett)	David Copperfield	11
Orange, Mr. and Mrs.	Holiday Romance	4
" Original Pig " ...	Mudfog Papers, 1st	
	Meeting	
Orlick, Dolge	Great Expectations	15
Our Next-Door Neigh-		
bour—" Boz " ...	Our Parish	7

Character or place.   *Book.*   *Chap.*

Overton, Joseph—
  " Boz " ... ...   Winglebury Duel
Overton, Mr.   ... ...   The Strange Gentleman

P

Packer, Tom   ... ...   Perils Of Certain
                              English Prisoners   1
Palaces, etc.   ... ...   Pictures From Italy
Pancks, Mr.   ... ...   Little Dorrit, Book 1   12
Pangloss   ... ...   Uncommercial Travel-
                              ler   8
Pankey, Miss   ... ...   Dombey And Son   8
Paolo, St.   ... ...   Pictures From Italy
" Papers " ... ...   Mugby Junction—Boy
                              At Mugby
Pardiggle, Mrs. Mr.
  and boys ... ...   Bleak House   8
Parish Surgeon ... ...   Oliver Twist   1
Parish Clerk   ... ...   Pickwick   17
Parker, Uncle   ... ...   Our Mutual Friend,
                              Book 1   5
Parkes, Phil   ... ...   Barnaby Rudge   1
Parkins   ... ...   Reprinted Pieces—
                              Our Bore
Parkins, Mrs.   ... ...   Reprinted Pieces—
                              Ghost Of Art
Parkle ... ...   Uncommercial Travel
                              ler   14

Character or place.	Book.	Chap.
Parksop, Brother ...	George Silverman's Explanation	6
Parma	Pictures From Italy	
Parsons, Gabriel and Mrs.—" Boz " ...	Watkins Tottle	
Parsons, Mrs.	Sketches, Young Couples—The Contradictory	
Parvis, Arson	Message From The Sea	2
Pasnidge, Mr.	David Copperfield	2
Passengers by Coach	Nicholas Nickleby	5
Pauper's Funeral ...	Oliver Twist	5
Pavilionstone	Reprinted Pieces— Out Of Town	
Pawkins, Major and Mrs.	Martin Chuzzlewit	16
Payne, Dr.	Pickwick	2
Peacoat	Reprinted Pieces— Down With the Tide	
Peacock, The	Pickwick	13
Peacocks	Holiday Romance	2
Peak	Barnaby Rudge	23
Peasants	Pictures From Italy	
Pebbleson, Nephew ...	No Thoroughfare— Act 1 : The Curtain Rises	
Pecksniff, Mr., Charity and Mercy	Martin Chuzzlewit	2
Peddle and Pool	Little Dorrit, Book 1	36
Peecher, Miss	Our Mutual Friend, Book 2	1

Character or place.	*Book.*	*Chap.*
Peepy, Miss	Reprinted Pieces— Our English Watering Place	
Peerybingle, John, Dot and Baby	Cricket on the Hearth; Chirp 1st	
Peffer	Bleak House	10
Pegasus's Arms	Hard Times, Book 1	6
Pegler, Mrs.	Hard Times, Book 2	6
Peggotty	David Copperfield	1
Peggotty, Ham	David Copperfield	1
Peggotty, Daniel ...	David Copperfield	3
Pell, Solomon	Pickwick	43
Penitentiary, Eastern	American Notes	7
Penrewen	Message From The Sea	2
Peplow, Mrs.—" Boz "	Streets By Night	
Peps, Parker, Dr. ...	Dombey And Son	1
Perch, Mr. and Mrs.	Dombey And Son	13
Percy, Lord	Barnaby Rudge	67
Perker, Mr.	Pickwick	10
Perkins, Mrs.	Bleak House	11
Perkins	Haunted House— Mortals In The House	
Perkinsop, Mary Ann	Mrs. Lirriper's Lodgings	1
Pessell and Mortair, ... Messrs.	Mudfog Papers, 2nd Meeting	
Peter, Lord—" Boz "	Winglebury Duel	
Peters, St.	Pictures From Italy	
Petowker, Miss	Nicholas Nickleby	14
Pettifer, Tom	Message From The Sea	1

Character or place.	*Book.*	*Chap.*
Phantom, The	Haunted Man	1
Phenomenon, Infant, The	'Nicholas Nickleby	23
Phibbs, Mr.	Reprinted Pieces— Detective Anecdotes	
Phil	Bleak House	21
" Phil "	Reprinted Pieces— Our School	
Philadelphia	American Notes	7
Phoebe	Nicholas Nickleby	11
Phoebe	Mugby Junction— Barbox Bros.	
Phunkey, Mr.	Pickwick	31
Physician	Little Dorrit, Book 1	21
Physician's daughter ...	Somebody's Luggage— His Boots	
Piacenza	Pictures From Italy	
Pickford	Uncommercial Travel- ler	12
Pickle, Mr. of Portici	Pictures From Italy	
Pickles	Holiday Romance	2
Pickleson	Dr. Marigold's Pre- scriptions	1
Picture Galleries of Rome	Pictures From Italy	
Pickwick, Mr. Samuel	Pickwick and Master Humphrey's Clock	3
Pidgeon, Mr. Thomas	Reprinted Pieces— Detective Police	
Pidger, Mr.	David Copperfield	41
Pierce, Capt. and daughters	Reprinted Pieces— Long Voyage	

Character or place.	*Book.*	*Chap.*
Piff, Miss	Mugby Junction—Boy at Mugby	
" Pig and Tinder Box "	Mudfog Papers, 1st Meeting	
Pike Boat	American Notes	12
Pilgrims Supper	Pictures From Italy	
Pilkins, Mr.	Dombey And Son	1
Pinch, Tom	Martin Chuzzlewit	2
Pinch, Ruth	Martin Chuzzlewit	9
Pip, Mr.	Martin Chuzzlewit	28
Pipchin, Mrs.	Dombey And Son	8
Piper, Mrs.	Bleak House	11
Piper, Professor	Martin Chuzzlewit	34
Pipkin, Mr.	Mudfog Papers, 2nd Meeting	
Pipkin, Nathaniel ...	Pickwick	17
Pipson	Haunted House—Ghost In Master B.'s Room	
Pirates	Perils Of Certain English Prisoners	1
Pirrip, Philip	Great Expectations	1
Pisa	Pictures From Italy	
Pitchlynn	American Notes	12
Pitt, Jane	Reprinted Pieces— Schoolboy's Story	
Pittsburgh	American Notes	10
Plea for Total Abstinence	Uncommercial Traveller	35
Plornish, Mr.	Little Dorrit, Book 1	9
Plornish, Mrs.	Little Dorrit, Book 1	12
Pluck, Mr.	Nicholas Nickleby	19

Character or place.	*Book.*	*Chap.*
Plummer, Caleb	Cricket On The Hearth Chirp 1st	
Plummer, Bertha ...	Cricket On The Hearth Chirp 2nd	
Plummer, Edward ...	Cricket On The Hearth Chirp 3rd	
Pocket, Herbert	Great Expectations	21
Pocket, Matthew, etc.	Great Expectations	11
Pocket, Mrs., Alec and Jane	Great Expectations	22
Pocket Breaches	Our Mutual Friend, Book 2	3
Podder	Pickwick	7
Podgers, Mr.	Lazy Tour Of Two Idle Apprentices	1
Poddles	Our Mutual Friend, Book 1	16
Podgers, John	Master Humphrey's Clock	3
Podsnap, Georgiana ...	Our Mutual Friend, Book 1	11
Podsnap, Mr. and Mrs.	Our Mutual Friend, Book 1	2
Pogram, Hon. Elijah	Martin Chuzzlewit	34
" Polly "	Mugby Junction— Barbox Bros. and Co.	
Polreath, David	Message From The Sea	2
Pompeii	Pictures From Italy	
Pope, The	Pictures From Italy	
Pordage, Commissioner	Perils Of Certain English Prisoners	1

Character or place.	*Book.*	*Chap.*
Porkenhams, The ...	Pickwick	25
Porkin and Snob ...	Pickwick	40
Porter, Mrs. J.—"Boz"	Mrs. Joseph Porter	
Porters, Foolish Mr.	Edwin Drood	3
Portuguese Captain ...	Perils Of Certain English Prisoners	1
Postillion	Pictures From Italy	
Pott, Mr. and Mrs. ...	Pickwick	13
Potter, Thomas— "Boz"	Making A Night Of It	
Potterson, Job	Our Mutual Friend, Book 1	3
Potterson, Miss Abbey	Our Mutual Friend, Book 1	6
Pratchett, Mrs.	Somebody's Luggage— Leaving It Till Called For	
Prentices	Bleak House	10
Prentice, Knights ...	Barnaby Rudge	8
Prerogative Office— "Boz"	Doctors Commons	
President, Lord	Barnaby Rudge	67
President, The	American Notes	8
President	Tale Of Two Cities, Book 3	6
Pressroom—"Boz" ...	Newgate	
Price, Mr.	Pickwick	40
Price, Matilda	Nicholas Nickleby	9
Priest, Old, The ...	Pictures From Italy	
Princess's Place	Dombey And Son	7
Prisons	American Notes	6

Character or place.	*Book.*	*Chap.*
Prisoners' Van, The —" Boz "	Characters	12
Prisoners— " Boz "	Newgate And Old Bailey	
Private Theatres— " Boz "	Scenes	13
Proctors—" Boz " ...	Doctors Commons	
Prodgit, Mrs.	Reprinted Pieces— Births	
Prosee, Mr.	Mudfog Papers, 2nd Meeting	
Prosee, Mr.	Pickwick	47
Pross, Miss and Her Brother Solomon ...	Tale Of Two Cities, Book 2	6
Provis	Great Expectations	40
Pruffle	Pickwick	39
Public Buildings, Boston	American Notes	3
Public Buildings, New York	American Notes	8
Public Buildings, St. Louis	American Notes	12
Public Dinners—"Boz"	Scenes	19
Pubsey and Co.	Our Mutual Friend, Book 2	5
Pugstyles, Mr.	Nicholas Nickleby	16
Pumblechook, Uncle ...	Great Expectations	4
Pumkinskull, Professor	Mudfog Papers, 2nd Meeting	
Pupford, Miss	Tom Tiddler's Ground	6
Pupford's, Miss, Assistant	Tom Tiddler's Ground	6

Character or place.	*Book.*	*Chap.*
Pupker, Sir Matthew	Nicholas Nickleby	2
Purblind, Mr.	Mudfog Papers, 2nd Meeting	
Purday, Capt.—" Boz "	Our Parish	4
Pyke, Mr.	Nicholas Nickleby	19

Q

Quadrille Party— " Boz "	New Year	
Quale, Mr.	Bleak House	4
Quebec	American Notes	15
Queenstown	American Notes	15
Queer Small Boy ...	Uncommercial Traveller	7
Queerspeck, Professor	Mudfog Papers, 1st Meeting	
Quickear	Uncommercial Traveller	5
Quilp, Daniel and Mrs.	Old Curiosity Shop	3
Quinch, Mrs. ...	Uncommercial Traveller	27
Quinion, Mr.	David Copperfield	2

R

Rachael, Mrs.	Bleak House	3
Rachael	Hard Times, Book 1	10
Raddle, Mr. and Mrs.	Pickwick	32
Radfoot, George ...	Our Mutual Friend, Book 2	12

Character or place.	Book.	Chap.
Rainbird, Alice	Holiday Romance	1
Rairyganoo, Sally ...	Mrs. Lirriper's Legacy	1
Rames, W.	Wreck of The Golden Mary—The Wreck	
Rarx, Mr	Wreck of The Golden Mary—The Wreck	
Rats Castle	Reprinted Pieces— On Duty, etc.	
Raven, The (Grip) ...	Barnaby Rudge	6
Raven at Monastery ...	Pictures From Italy	
Ravender, Capt	Wreck of The Golden Mary—The Wreck	
Raybrock, Mrs., Alfred and Hugh	Message From The Sea	1
Raymond Cousin ...	Great Expectations	11
Recruiting Sergeant ...	Barnaby Rudge	31
Redburn Jack ...	Master Humphrey's Clock	2
Red Whisker	David Copperfield	33
Redforth	Holiday Romance	1
Redlaw, Mr	Haunted Man	1
Refractories	Uncommercial Traveller	3
Refreshments for Travellers	Uncommercial Traveller	6
Registrar—" Boz." ...	Doctors Commons	
Reporters—" Boz." ...	The House	
Reverend, The	Reprinted Pieces— Schoolboy's Story	
Riah	Our Mutual Friend, Book 2	5

Character or place.	*Book.*	*Chap.*
Richard	The Chimes	1
Richards (Mrs Toodles)	Dombey And Son	2
Richmond	American Notes	9
Riderhood, Rogue ...	Our Mutual Friend, Book 1	6
Riderhood, Pleasant ...	Our Mutual Friend, Book 2	12
Rigaud	Little Dorrit, Book 1	1
River, The—"Boz."	Scenes	10
River Steamboats ...	American Notes	9
Rob the Grinder ...	Dombey And Son	2
Robinson—"Boz." ...	Our Parish	3
Robinson—"Boz." ...	Boarding House	1
Rochester	Pickwick, and Seven Poor Travellers	2
Rockingham, Lord ...	Barnaby Rudge	67
Rodgers, Mrs	Pickwick	46
Rodgers, Mr	Reprinted Pieces— Long Voyage	
Rogers—"Boz." ...	The Parlour Orator	
Roker, Tom, Mr. ...	Pickwick	41
Rokesmith, John ...	Our Mutual Friend, Book 1	4
Rome	Pictures From Italy	
Rosa	Bleak House	7
Rose	Village Coquettes	
Rouncewell, Mrs ...	Bleak House	7
Rouncewell, George ...	Bleak House	7
Rouncewell, Watt ...	Bleak House	7
Royal George, Dover	Tale Of Two Cities, Book 1	4

Character or place.	Book.	Chap.
Rudge	Barnaby Rudge	1
Rudge, Barnaby	Barnaby Rudge	3
Rudge, Mrs	Barnaby Rudge	4
Ruffian, The	Uncommercial Traveller	36
Rugg, Mr and Miss ...	Little Dorrit, Book 1	25
Rummun, Professor ...	Mudfog Papers, 2nd Meeting	

S

Sacristan, The	Pictures From Italy	
Saggers, Mrs	Uncommercial Traveller	27
Salcy, Monsr. P. and family	Uncommercial Traveller	25
Salem House	David Copperfield	5
Sally	No Thoroughfare— The Overture	
Sampson, Mr	Hunted Down	2
Sampson, George ...	Our Mutual Friend, Book 1	4
Samson	Tale of Two Cities, Book 3	9
San Carlo	Pictures From Italy	
Sanders, Mrs.	Pickwick	26
Sandusky	American Notes	14
Sans Sebastiano	Pictures From Italy	
Sapsea, Mr. Thomas ...	Edwin Drood	4
Saracen's Head, Towcester	Pickwick	51

Character or place.	*Book.*	*Chap.*
Saracen's Head, Snow Hill	Nicholas Nickleby	3
Sarah—" Boz "	Our Parish	2
Satis House	Great Expectations	8
Savage, The Noble ...	Reprinted Pieces	
Saville, Lord	Barnaby Rudge	73
Saunders	Sketches, Young Couples—Couple Who Dote On Their Children	
Sawyer, Bob	Pickwick	30
Sawyer, Mr	Mr. Robert Bolton	
Scadder, Mr	Martin Chuzzlewit	21
Scadgers, Lady	Hard Times, Book 1	7
Scaley and Tix	Nicholas Nickleby	21
Schoolmaster—" Boz "	Our Parish	1
Schoolmaster	Old Curiosity Shop	24
Schutz, Mr	Reprinted Pieces— Long Voyage	
Scientific Gent	Pickwick	39
Scotland Yard—" Boz."	Scenes	4
Scott, Tom	Old Curiosity Shop	50
Screw Packet	Martin Chuzzlewit	15
Scrooge, Ebenezer and nephew	Christmas Carol, Stave 1	
Scrooge's niece and sisters	Christmas Carol, Stave 3	
Seamstress, Little, The	Tale Of Two Cities, Book 3	13
Seraglio	Haunted House—Ghost In Master B.'s Room	
Seraphina, Lady ...	Little Dorrit, Book 1	17

Character or place.	Book.	Chap.
Seraph, The...	Martin Chuzzlewit	9
Sergeant and Soldiers	Great Expectations	5
Servant	The Lamplighter	
Servant, John	Is She His Wife?	
Servant, Little, at Brasses	Old Curiosity Shop	34
Seven-Dials—" Boz."	Scenes	5
Sexton, The	Old Curiosity Shop	53
Sexton, The	Little Dorrit, Book 1	14
Shabby-Genteel People —" Boz."	Characters	10
Shaker Village	American Notes	15
Sharp, Mr	David Copperfield	6
Sharpeye	Uncommercial Traveller	5
Shepherd, Miss ...	David Copperfield	18
Short-Timers, The	Uncommercial Traveller	29
Shy Neighbourhoods	Uncommercial Traveller	10
Siena	Pictures From Italy	
Signalman and spectre	Mugby Junction—No. 1 Branch Line	
Silvia	George Silverman's Explanation	5
Simmery, Mr	Pickwick	55
Simmonds, Mrs ...	Old Curiosity Shop	4
Simmons—" Boz." ...	Our Parish	1
Simmons, Bill	Martin Chuzzlewit	13
Simpson	Pickwick	42
Simpson—" Boz." ...	The Boarding House	1

Character or place.	Book.	Chap.
Simson—" Boz."	The Steam Excursion	
Single Gentleman	Old Curiosity Shop	34
Skettles, Sir Barnet	Dombey And Son	14
Skettles, Lady and Master	Dombey And Son	14
Skewton, Mrs	Dombey And Son	21
Skiffins, Miss	Great Expectations	37
Skimpin, Mr.	Pickwick	34
Skimpole, Harold	Bleak House	6
Skimpole, Mrs. and daughters	Bleak House	43
Slackbridge	Hard Times, Book 2	4
Slammer, Dr	Pickwick	2
Slang, Lord	Sketches, Young Couples—The Egotistical	
Slaughter, Lieutenant —" Boz."	Tuggs's At Ramsgate	
Slavery	American Notes	17
Sleary, Josephine	Hard Times, Book 1	3
Sleary, Mr	Hard Times, Book 1	6
Sliderskew, Peg	Nicholas Nickleby	51
Slinkton, Julius	Hunted Down	2
Slithers, Mr	Master Humphrey's Clock	5
Sliverstone, Mr and Mrs	Sketches, Young Couples—The Egotistical	
Sloppy	Our Mutual Friend, Book 1	16
Slout, Mr	Oliver Twist	27

Character or place.	Book.	Chap.
Slowboy, Tilly	Cricket On The Hearth	1
Sluffen, Mr.—" Boz "	Scenes	20
Slug, Mr	Mudfog Papers, 1st Meeting	
Slum	Old Curiosity Shop	28
Slumkey, Hon. S. ...	Pickwick	13
Slummery, Mr. ...	Sketches, Young Couples —The Plausible	
Slurk, Mr	Pickwick	51
Slyme, Chevy	Martin Chuzzlewit	4
Smallweed, Bart ...	Bleak House	20
Smallweed, Grandfather, Mrs and Judy	Bleak House	21
Smangle	Pickwick	41
Smart Tom	Pickwick	14
Smauker, John	Pickwick	37
Smiff, Putman	Martin Chuzzlewit	22
Smike	Nicholas Nickleby	8
Smith, Mr—" Boz."	The House	
Smith, Mr	Mudfog Papers, 2nd Meeting	
Smiths—" Boz." ...	Mrs. J. Porter	
Smithers, Emily— " Boz."	Sentiment	
Smithers, Robert— " Boz."	Making A Night Of It	
Smithick and Watersby	Wreck of The Golden Mary—The Wreck	
Smithies, The	Pickwick	2
Smorltork, Count ...	Pickwick	15

Character or place.	Book.	Chap.
Smouch	Pickwick	40
Smuggins—" Boz."	Streets By Night	
Snagsby, Mr. and Mrs	Bleak House	10
Snap, Betsy	Reprinted Pieces—Poor Relation's Story	
Snawley and boys ...	Nicholas Nickleby	4
Snewkes, Mr.	Nicholas Nickleby	14
Snevellicci, Miss ...	Nicholas Nickleby	23
Snevellicci, Mr. and Mrs	Nicholas Nickleby	30
Snicks	Pickwick	47
Sniff, Mr and Mrs ...	Mugby Junction—Boy At Mugby	
Sniggle and Blink ...	Pickwick	40
Sniggs, Mr	Mudfog Papers—Life of Mr. Tulrumble	
Snigsworthy, Lord ...	Our Mutual Friend, Book 1	2
Snipes, The...	Pickwick	2
Snitchey, Mr	Battle Of Life, Part 1st	
Snitchey, Mrs	Battle Of Life, Part 2nd	
Snittle Timberry, Mr	Nicholas Nickleby	48
Snobb	Nicholas Nickleby	19
Snodgrass, Augustus	Pickwick	1
Snore, Professor ...	Mudfog Papers, 1st Meeting	
Snorflerer, Lady ...	Sketches, Young Couples—The Egotistical	
Snow, Tom	Wreck of The Golden Mary--The Wreck	

Character or place.	*Book.*	*Chap.*
Snubbin, Sergeant ...	Pickwick	31
Snuggery, The	Pickwick	42
Snuggery	Little Dorrit, Book 1	8
Snuffim, Sir Tumley	Nicholas Nickleby	21
Snuffletoffle, Mr ...	Mudfog Papers, 2nd Meeting	
Snuphanuph, Lady ...	Pickwick	35
Soemup, Dr	Mudfog Papers, 2nd Meeting	
Solicitor General ...	Tale Of Two Cities, Book 2	3
Sophy	Dr. Marigold's Prescriptions	1
Sowster	Mudfog Papers, 2nd Meeting	
Sowerberry, Mr and Mrs	Oliver Twist	4
Sowndes, Mr	Dombey And Son	31
Sparkes, Tom	The Strange Gentleman	
Sparkins, Horatio— " Boz "	Horatio Sparkins	
Sparkler, Edmund ...	Little Dorrit, Book 1	21
Sparsit, Mrs.	Hard Times, Book 1	7
Spatter, John	Reprinted Pieces— Poor Relation's Story	
Specks, Joe and family	Uncommercial Traveller	12
Spectre	Haunted House—Ghost In Master B.'s Room	
Speddie, Dr.	Lazy Tour Of Two Idle Apprentices	2

Character or place.	Book.	Chap.
Speechless Friend, The	No Thoroughfare—Act 2 : Vendale Makes Love	
Spenlow, Mr.	David Copperfield	23
Spenlow, Dora	David Copperfield	26
Spenlow, Misses ...	David Copperfield	41
Spezzia	Pictures From Italy	
Spiker, Henry, Mr. and Mrs.	David Copperfield	25
Spitfire	Dombey and Son	3
Spottletoe, Mr. and Mrs.	Martin Chuzzlewit	4
Spruggins, Mr. and Mrs.—" Boz " ...	Our Parish	4
Sprodgkin, Mrs. ...	Our Mutual Friend, Book 4	11
Spyers, Jem	Oliver Twist	31
Squeers, Mr. and Wackford	Nicholas Nickleby	3
Squeers, Mrs.	Nicholas Nickleby	7
Squeers, Miss Fanny	Nicholas Nickleby	9
Squires, Olympia ...	Uncommercial Traveller	19
Squod, Phil	Bleak House	24
St. Louis	American Notes	12
St. Stefans Rotondo ...	Pictures From Italy	
Stables, Hon. Bob ...	Bleak House	2
Stage Coaches	American Notes, 9 and 14	
Stagg	Barnaby Rudge	8
Staggs' Gardens	Dombey And Son	6
Stalker, Inspector ...	Reprinted Pieces— Detective Police	

Character or place.	Book.	Chap.
Staple, Mr.	Pickwick	7
Stareleigh, Justice ...	Pickwick	34
Stargazer, Mr., Master Gallileo, and Emma	The Lamplighter	
Starling, Mrs.	Sketches, Young Couples—The Loving	
Starling, Alfred and wife	Haunted House—Mortals In The House	
Startop	Great Expectations	23
Steadiman, John	Wreck Of The Golden Mary—The Wreck	
Steamboats, Fulton and St. Louis	American Notes	12
Steepways	Message From The Sea	1
Steerforth, James ...	David Copperfield	6
Steerforth, Mrs. ...	David Copperfield	20
Stiggins, Mr.	Pickwick	27
Stiltstalkings, The ...	Little Dorrit, Book 1	10
Stiltstalking, Lord Lancaster	Little Dorrit, Book 1	26
Stokes	Village Coquettes	
Stonebreaker	Uncommercial Traveller	22
Stone Lodge	Hard Times, Book 1	3
Strasburgh	Uncommercial Traveller	7
Strange Gentleman ...	The Strange Gentleman	
Straudenheim	Uncommercial Traveller	7
Straw, Sergeant ...	Reprinted Pieces—Detective Police	

Character or place.	Book.	Chap.
Streaker	Haunted House—Mortals In The House	
Strollers Tale, The	Pickwick	3
Strong, Dr. and Mrs. Annie	David Copperfield	16
Struggles	Pickwick	7
Stryver, Mr.	Tale Of Two Cities, Book 2	3
Stryver, Mrs.	Tale Of Two Cities, Book 2	21
Stubbs, Mrs.—" Boz "	The Steam Excursion	
Stumps, Bill	Pickwick	11
Stumpy and Deacon	Pickwick	40
Summerson, Esther	Bleak House	3
Superintendent, Mr.	Uncommercial Traveller	5
Sweedlepipe, Paul	Martin Chuzzlewit	26
Sweeney, Mrs.	Uncommercial Traveller	14
Swidger, Mr. and Mrs., William and Phillip	Haunted Man	1
Swidger, George	Haunted Man	2
Swills, Little	Bleak House	11
Switzerland	Pictures From Italy	
Swiveller, Dick	Old Curiosity Shop	2
Swosser, Capt.	Bleak House	13
Sikes, Bill and dog	Oliver Twist	13

T

| Table Rock | American Notes | 15 |

Character or place.	*Book.*	*Chap.*
Tablewick, Mrs. ...	Sketches, Young Couples—The Plausible	
Tacker	Martin Chuzzlewit	19
Tackleton, Mr.	Cricket On The Hearth, Chirp 1st	
Tadger, Brother ...	Pickwick	33
Tally-Ho Thompson	Reprinted Pieces—Detective Police	
Tangle, Mr.	Bleak House	1
Tape	Reprinted Pieces—Prince Bull	
Tapkins, Felix	Is She His Wife?	
Tapley, Mark	Martin Chuzzlewit	5
Taplin, Mr.—" Boz "	The Mistaken Milliner	
Tappertit, Simon ...	Barnaby Rudge	4
Tappleton, Lieutenant	Pickwick	2
Tartar, Bob	Reprinted Pieces—Schoolboy's Story	
Tartar, Mr.	Edwin Drood	17
Tatham, Mr.—" Boz."	Pawnbroker's Shop	
Tatt, Mr.	Reprinted Pieces—Detective Anecdotes	
Tattycoram	Little Dorrit, Book 1	2
Tauntons, The—" Boz "	Steam Excursion	
Taunton, Capt., and mother	Seven Poor Travellers	1
Taylor, Mr.	American Notes	3
Tea Gardens—" Boz "	London Recreations	
Tellsons Bank	Tale of Two Cities, Book 1	2

Character or place.	*Book.*	*Chap.*
Temeraire	Uncommercial Traveller	32
Testator, Mr.	Uncommercial Traveller	14
Tetterbys, Mr., Mrs. and family	Haunted Man	2
Theatres	American Notes	3
Theophile, Corporal ...	Somebody's Luggage— His Boots	
Thickness, Mr. ...	Mr. Robert Bolton	
Thompson, Julia ...	Sketches, Young Gents— The Domestic	
Thompson, Mrs. ...	Sketches, Young Gents— The Censorious	
Thomson, Sir John— " Boz "	The House	
Tibbs, Mr. and Mrs.— " Boz "	The Boarding House	1
Tickle, Mr.	Mudfog Papers, 2nd Meeting	
Tickit, Mrs.	Little Dorrit, Book 1	16
Tiddypot	Reprinted Pieces— Our Vestry	
Tiffey	David Copperfield	26
Tigg, Montague, Mr.	Martin Chuzzlewit	4
Timbered, Mr. ...	Mudfog Papers, 1st Meeting	
Timberry, Mr. Snittle	Nicholas Nickleby	48
Timkins—" Boz " .	The Parish	4
Timpsons	Uncommercial Traveller	12

Character or place.	*Book.*	*Chap.*
Timson, Rev.—'' Boz ''	Watkins Tottle	
Tinker, Travelling ...	Oliver Twist	28
Tinker, The	Tom Tiddler's Ground	1
Tinkler, Mr.	Little Dorrit, Book 2	5
Tinkling, William ...	Holiday Romance	1
Tiny Tim	Christmas Carol, Stave	3
Tipkisson	Reprinted Pieces—	
	Our Hon. Friend	
Tipp	David Copperfield	11
Tippin family, The—		
'' Boz ''	Tuggs's At Ramsgate	
Tippins, Lady	Our Mutual Friend,	
	Book 1	2
Tisher, Mrs.	Edwin Drood	3
Tix, Mr.	Nicholas Nickleby	21
Toddles	Our Mutual Friend,	
	Book 1	16
Todds' Young Man—		
'' Boz ''	Streets By Morning	
Toddyhigh, Joe ...	Master Humphrey's	
	Clock	1
Todgers, Mrs.	Martin Chuzzlewit	8
Tom	Nicholas Nickleby	16
Tom	Somebody's Luggage—	
	His Brown Paper	
	Parcel	
Tom	Tale Of Two Cities,	
	Book 1	2
Tombs, New York ...	American Notes	6
Tomkins, Miss	Pickwick	16
Tomkins	Nicholas Nickleby	13

Character or place.	Book.	Chap.
Tomkins, Charles ...	The Strange Gentleman	
Tomkins—" Boz " ...	The Boarding House	2
Toodles and family ...	Dombey And Son	2
Toorell, Dr.	Mudfog Papers, 1st Meeting	
Toozellem, Hon. C. ...	Little Dorrit, Book 1	17
Tootle, Tom	Our Mutual Friend, Book 1	6
Tootleum Boots ...	Holiday Romance	4
Toots, Mr.	Dombey And Son	11
Tope, Mr. and Mrs. ...	Edwin Drood	2
Topper	Christmas Carol	3
Tottle, Watkins— " Boz."	Watkins Tottle	
Toppet, Miss	Martin Chuzzlewit	34
Toronto	American Notes	15
Tozer	Dombey And Son	12
Towlinson	Dombey And Son	5
Town Arms, Eatanswill	Pickwick	13
Tox, Miss	Dombey And Son	1
Tpschoffki, Major ...	House To Let—Going Into Society	
Trabb and Boy	Great Expectations	19
Traddles, Tommy ...	David Copperfield	6
Trampfoot	Uncommercial Traveller	5
Tramps	Uncommercial Traveller	11
Traveller, Mr.	Tom Tiddler's Ground	1
Travellers, Twopenny	Edwin Drood	5

11

Character or place	Book.	Chap.
Travelling Abroad ...	Uncommercial Traveller	7
Treasury	Little Dorrit, Book 1	21
Tredgear, John	Message From The Sea	2
Tregarthen	Message From The Sea	2
Trent, Fred	Old Curiosity Shop	2
Tresham	Mugby Junction—Barbox Bros. and Co.	
Trimmers, Mr.	Nicholas Nickleby	35
Trinkle, Mr.	Reprinted Pieces—Detective Anecdotes	
Trotter, Job	Pickwick	16
Trott, A. Esq.—"Boz"	Winglebury Duel	
Trotwood, Betsy ...	David Copperfield	1
Truck, Mr.	Mudfog Papers, 1st Meeting	
Trundle, Mr.	Pickwick	4
Tuckle, Mr. (Blazes)	Pickwick	37
Tugby, Mr.	The Chimes, 4th quarter	
Tuggs's The—"Boz"	Tuggs's At Ramsgate	
Tulkinghorn, Mr. ...	Bleak House	2
Tulrumble, Mr., Mrs. and Son	Mudfog Papers—Life Of Mr. Tulrumble	
Tungay	David Copperfield	6
Tupman, Tracey, Mr.	Pickwick	1
Tupple, Mr.—"Boz."	The New Year	
Turnpike Keeper, The	Uncommercial Traveller	22
Turveydrop, Mr. ...	Bleak House	14

Character or place	*Book.*	*Chap.*
Turveydrop, Prince ...	Bleak House	14
Tuscan, The	Pictures From Italy	
Twemlow, Mr.	Our Mutual Friend, Book 1	2
Twickenham	Little Dorrit, Book 1	16
Twigger, Mr. and Mrs.	Mudfog Papers—Life of Mr. Tulrumble	
Twinkleton, Miss ...	Edwin Drood	3
Twist Oliver	Oliver Twist	1
Two Robins Inn ...	Lazy Tour Of Two Idle Apprentices	2

U

Ugly Old Man	David Copperfield	13
Undery, Mr.	Haunted House—Mortals In The House	
United Metropolitan Muffin Co.	Nicholas Nickleby	2

V

Valentine, Private ...	Somebody's Luggage—His Boots	
Valmontone, Inn at ...	Pictures From Italy	
Vatican, The	Pictures From Italy	
Varden, Gabriel	Barnaby Rudge	2
Varden, Mrs. and Dolly	Barnaby Rudge	3
Veck, Toby	The Chimes, 1st quarter	

Character or place	*Book.*	*Chap.*
Veiled Lady, The ...	No Thoroughfare— The Overture	
Vendale, George ...	No Thoroughfare— Act 1 : The House- keeper Speaks	
Veneering, Mr. and Mrs. and baby ...	Our Mutual Friend, Book 1	2
Vengeance, The	Tale of Two Cities, Book 2	22
Venice	Pictures From Italy	
Venning, Mrs.	Perils Of Certain English Prisoners	1
Ventriloquist	Uncommercial Travel- ler	25
Venus, Mr.	Our Mutual Friend, Book 1	7
Verbosity, Member for	Reprinted Pieces— Our Hon Member	
Verisopht, Lord	Nicholas Nickleby	19
Verity, Mr.	George Silverman's Explanation	4
Verona	Pictures From Italy	
Vestry-clerk " Boz "	Our Parish	1
Vesuvius	Pictures From Italy	
Vholes, Mr.	Bleak House	37
Vholes, The Misses ...	Bleak House	37
Villagers, The	Tale Of Two Cities, Book 2	8
Voigt, Maitre	No Thoroughfare— Act 4 : The Clock Lock	

Character or place.	*Book.*	*Chap.*
Volumnia	Bleak House	28
Voyage Out	American Notes	1 and 2
Voyage Home	American Notes	16
Vuffin	Old Curiosity Shop	?9

W

Wackles, Sophy	Old Curiosity Shop	7
Wackles, Mrs. and her other daughters ...	Old Curiosity Shop	8
Wade, Miss	Little Dorrit, Book 1	2
Waghorn, Mr.	Mudfog Papers, 1st Meeting	
Waiter at Yarmouth	David Copperfield	5
Waiter at the Golden Cross	David Copperfield	19
Waiters	The Strange Gentleman	
Waitress, The	Uncommercial Traveller	22
Wakefields, The " Boz "	Steam Excursion	
Walker, Mick	David Copperfield	11
Walker, Mrs.— " Boz "	Streets By Night	
Walker, Mr.— " Boz"	Watkins Tottle	
Walmers, Mr. and Harry	Holly Tree Inn—Boots	
Walter M'Neville " Boz "	Sentiment	

Character or place	*Book.*	*Chap.*
Wapping Workhouse	Uncommercial Travel-ler	3
Warden, Michael ...	Battle Of Life	2
Wardle, Mr. and family	Pickwick	4
Wardle, Old Mrs. ...	Pickwick	6
Warren, The	Barnaby Rudge	1
Washington	American Notes	8
Waterbrook, Mr. and Mrs.	David Copperfield	25
Watertoast Gazette ...	Martin Chuzzlewit	21
Waters, Capt. and Mrs.—" Boz." ...	Tuggs's at Ramsgate	
Watkins, King and Queen	Holiday Romance	2
Watsons, The	Sketches Young Gents— The Very Friendly	
Watts, Richard	Seven Poor Travellers	1
Wedgington, Mrs. B.	Reprinted Pieces— Out Of The Season	
Weevle, Mr.	Bleak House	20
Wegg, Silas	Our Mutual Friend, Book 1	5
Weller, Sam	Pickwick and Master Humphrey's Clock	10 3
Weller, Mr. Senr. ...	Pickwick and Master Humphrey's Clock	20 3
Weller, Mrs.	Pickwick	27
Wemmick	Great Expectations	20

Character or place	*Book.*	*Chap.*
Westlock, John	Martin Chuzzlewit	2
Westgate House School	Pickwick	16
Wharton Granville, Mr.	George Silverman's Explanation	9
Wheezy, Professor ...	Mudfog Papers, 1st Meeting	
Whiff, Miss	Mugby Junction—Boy At Mugby	
Whiffler, Mr. and Mrs.	Sketches, Young Couples—The Couple Who Dote On Their Children	
Whiffers, Mr.	Pickwick	37
Whimple, Mrs. ...	Great Expectations	46
White	Holiday Romance	4
White House	American Notes	8
White Hart, Bath	Pickwick	35
White Hart, Borough	Pickwick	10
Whisker	Old Curiosity Shop	14
Wickfield, Mr. and Agnes	David Copperfield	15
Wickham, Mrs.	Dombey And Son	8
Wicks, Mr.	Pickwick	20
Widger, Bobtail, Mr. and Mrs.	Sketches, Young Couples—The Plausible	
Wield, Inspector ...	Reprinted Pieces—Detective Police	
Wigsby, Mr.	Reprinted Pieces—Our Vestry	
Wigsby, Mr.	Mudfog Papers, 1st Meeting	

Character or place	Book.	Chap.
Wilding, Walter ...	No Thoroughfare— The Overture	
Wilfer family	Our Mutual Friend, Book 1	4
Wilkins, Mr. Samuel— " Boz "	Miss Evans And The Eagle	
Wilkins, Dick	Christmas Carol, Stave 2	
Wilkins	Pickwick	19
Willet, John	Barnaby Rudge	1
Willet, Joe	Barnaby Rudge	1
Williams, William ...	Our Mutual Friend, Book 1	6
William, Sweet	Old Curiosity Shop	19
William, Coachman ...	David Copperfield	19
William, Shiney and others	Pickwick	5
Williamson, Mrs. ... " Boz "	Winglebury Duel	
Willing Mind, The ...	David Copperfield	3
Willing, Sophy	Mrs. Lirriper's Lodgings	1
Willis, The Misses— " Boz "	Our Parish	3
Willis—" Boz "	Watkins Tottle	
Wilson, Caroline— " Boz "	Sentiment	
Wilson, Mary and Fanny	The Strange Gentleman	
Wilson—" Boz." ...	The Parlour Orator	
Winglebury Arms— " Boz "	Winglebury Duel	

Character or place	*Book.*	*Chap.*
Winkle, Nathaniel, Esq	Pickwick	1
Winkle, Mr., senr. ...	Pickwick	50
Wisbottle, Mr.—		
" Boz "	The Boarding House	2
Wisk, Miss	Bleak House	30
Wizzle, Mr.—" Boz "	The Steam Excursion	
Witchem, Sergeant ...	Reprinted Pieces—	
	Detective Police	
Withers, Luke	Old Curiosity Shop	29
Withers	Dombey And Son	21
Witherden, Mr. ...	Old Curiosity Shop	14
Witherfield, Miss ...	Pickwick	24
Wititterly, Mr. and		
Mrs.	Nicholas Nickleby	21
Wobbler	Little Dorrit, Book 1	10
Wolf, Mr.	Martin Chuzzlewit	28
Woodcourt, Allan ...	Bleak House	14
Woodcourt, Mrs. ...	Bleak House	17
Woodenconse, Mr. ...	Mudfog Papers, 1st	
	Meeting	
Woodsawyer	Tale of Two Cities,	
	Book 3	5
Wopsle, Mr.	Great Expectations	4
Wopsles, Mr., Great		
Aunt	Great Expectations	7
Worcester	American Notes	5
Workhouse, Master—		
" Boz "	Our Parish	1
Workman	Dombey And Son	14
Wosky, Dr.—" Boz "	The Boarding House	2

Printed by F. J. Mansfield Erith S.E.